Precarious Constructions

Precarious Constructions

Race, Class, and Urban Revitalization in Toronto

Vanessa A. Rosa

The University of North Carolina Press CHAPEL HILL

Set in Merope Basic by Westchester Publishing Services
Manufactured in the United States of America

Library of Congress Cataloging-in-Publication Data
Names: Rosa, Vanessa A., author.
Title: Precarious constructions : race, class, and urban revitalization in
    Toronto / Vanessa A. Rosa.
Description: Chapel Hill : The University of North Carolina Press, 2023. |
    Includes bibliographical references and index.
Identifiers: LCCN 2023014309 | ISBN 9781469675756 (cloth ; alk. paper) |
    ISBN 9781469675763 (paperback ; alk. paper) | ISBN 9781469675770 (ebook)
Subjects: LCSH: Public housing—Ontario—Toronto. | Gentrification—
    Ontario—Toronto. | Housing policy—Ontario—Toronto—Citizen
    participation. | City planning—Ontario—Toronto. | Racism—Ontario—
    Toronto. | Regent Park (Toronto, Ont.)—Economic conditions. | Lawrence
    Heights (Toronto, Ont.)—Economic conditions. | Toronto (Ont.)—Ethnic
    relations. | BISAC: SOCIAL SCIENCE / Ethnic Studies / American /
    General | SOCIAL SCIENCE / Sociology / Urban
Classification: LCC HD7305.T68 R573 2023 | DDC 353.5/509713541—
    dc23/eng/20230503
LC record available at https://lccn.loc.gov/2023014309

Cover illustration by David Flores Design.

For my parents,
Gilbert and Kathleen Rosa

———

I hope you hear inside my voice of sorrow
And that it motivates you to make a better tomorrow
This place is cruel, nowhere could be much colder
If we don't change, the world will soon be over
Living just enough, stop giving just enough for the city
—STEVIE WONDER, "Living for the City"

Contents

Acknowledgments

This project would not have been possible without the generous support and encouragement of the dynamic and committed team at the University of North Carolina Press. Shout out to Dylan White for seeing the potential in this project and leaving my work in good hands with UNC Press. To my editor, Lucas Church, I am grateful for your patience and thoughtfulness along the way. Thanks to Thomas Bedenbaugh, Valerie Burton, Elizabeth Orange Lane, and Dino Battista for helping me make it through the home stretch and for managing every detail.

The pages that follow are informed by two beautiful communities in Toronto that welcomed me with open arms (and sometimes skepticism!). To them I say thank you for letting me sit, listen, learn, and think alongside you. Special appreciation to the women at the Regent Park Learning Center and former director, Abdu, who invited me in as a colearner and pushed me to expand my understanding of being in community. Many thanks to the City of Toronto planners and Toronto Community Housing Corporation (TCHC) representatives who took the time to meet with me and share their insights.

Beyond the gracious residents and organizations in Regent Park and Lawrence Heights, I am fortunate to be surrounded by various communities across borders that have sustained me.

This book has greatly benefited from the mentorship and training I received at the University of Toronto and York University. Stefan Kipfer, Radhika Mongia, Michael Nijhawan, and Sherene Razack, I could not have asked for better teachers and guides. I am forever grateful. Many thanks to Liette Gilbert for reading and offering feedback on early drafts of the first two chapters.

Much gratitude to my students at Mount Holyoke College who gave me space to think through different iterations of the arguments in this book. I am grateful for my brilliant research assistants Camila Blanco and Cindie Huerta, who read multiple drafts and worked diligently on citations. Mount Holyoke College also offered various forms of research support for which I am grateful. Thanks to Cathy Luna for helping me develop and edit the manuscript proposal and to Kate Epstein of Epstein Words for editorial guidance.

To Usamah Ansari, Antonio Nieves Martinez, and Eliatha Nicolau Georgeiou, my dear friends I lost along the way: You each held me up throughout the writing of this book. May you continue to rest in love and power.

I am indebted to my many colleagues and friends at Mount Holyoke College, the Five College Consortium, the New England Consortium for Latino Studies, and beyond. You have offered warmth, collegiality, and humor during the writing process. Special thanks to Llana Barber, Alan Bloomgarden, Kimberly Juanita Brown, Ginetta Candelario, Meredith Coleman-Tobias, Lorena Garcia, Teresa Gonzalez, Serin Houston, Ren-yo Hwang, Jackson Matos, Elliot Montague, Dorothy Mosby, Caro Pinto, Preston Smith, Sarah Stefana Smith, Maria Salgado-Cartagena, Alberto Sandoval-Sánchez, Ana K. Soltero-López, Mérida Rúa, Lucas Wilson, and Wes Yu. To Mari Castañeda, Iyko Day, David Hernández, and Joseph Krupcynski, you are models of true mentorship. Being in community together has been a grounding force as this project moved through its many phases. Mil gracias.

In Toronto and Massachusetts, I have been surrounded by a wellspring of love and friendship that helped when I was stuck and rallied to celebrate milestones along the way. Deepest appreciation to Dale Jordan, Rana Jordan, Rouba Jordan, Kristina McCarter, Alma Obeid, Amelia Williams, and Steve Williams. It was an honor and a life-changing experience to be able to work alongside and learn from Deena Ladd, Becky McFarlane, and Olivia Nuamah—you have each impacted communities in Toronto in immeasurable ways. Your sprinkles of wisdom stayed with me as I finished this book. Thank you to my people who helped make the valley feel like home and gave me time to pause, think, and laugh: Mary Jane Dean, Joel Arce, Kristin Woods, the Russo family, Eliza Rosewood, Luke Woodward, and Dori Midnight. My partners in liberation at Pa'lante Transformative Justice, Springfield No One Leaves, and the Holyoke Ethnic Studies Program completely shifted and strengthened the arguments in this book in ways I had not anticipated. Thank you.

Thanks to David Flores not only for the cover art, but for modeling what it means to envision beauty and art in a sometimes dark world and in the face of injustice. You inspire me.

To my teachers, mentors, and best friends, Kathryn Trevenen and Paul Saurette, you have been constant anchors along the way—including providing me with a home for many writing retreats, hundreds of cups of tea, and reading multiple drafts of this work. You have impacted my life in immeasurable ways—this book would not exist if it weren't for your love, mentorship, and friendship.

I am thankful for the two most important young people in my life, Izabella and Caleb, who encourage me to think about the possibilities of brighter futures.

My brothers, Jonathan and Gilbert, have been my solid coconspirators since day one. Gil, my marathon partner in crime — running together is the perfect metaphor for our relationship. I know whenever I look over my shoulder, you'll be right by my side as you have been during this arduous writing process. Special thanks to Jonathan, who read and offered feedback on each draft, provided editorial humor and shade in only the way a sibling could, helped me brainstorm the title, and offered insight to refine the introduction. I am beyond grateful for your patience, love, and nudging me to keep my energy going as I crossed the finish line with final edits. The best gift Mom and Dad gave us is each other.

Much gratitude and love to my partner and best friend, Nigel, who held me up in the writing process by listening to me ramble, reading page proofs, and making me laugh during the long journey of finishing this book. Your humor and generosity combined with your endless optimism and love make *every* aspect of this life so much better. Thank you.

Finally, it was my parents' curiosity and many tours through Toronto and New York City that ignited my own inquisitiveness about all things urban. My father grew up in public housing in Harlem and my mother in subsidized housing on the border of Regent Park in Toronto. My father would take me on tours of Harlem, noting how he watched his own building be torn down during slum clearance and his annoyance at the emergence of big box stores in his old neighborhood. One of my favorite memories is of how he would narrate the class divides from corner to corner and block to block as we drove through Harlem. He wondered out loud how poverty and wealth lived side by side, as if such abundance and deprivation were natural or neutral social facts. I am quite sure he knew the answers to his ponderings. My mother, similarly, loved taking us to Toronto, even though returning home was accompanied by the pain and trauma of remembering growing up in the midst of much instability. Her favorite place to take me in Toronto was the Allan Gardens, which were just a few blocks from where she grew up. She told me that as a young child she would bring her books to the gardens and sit and read as an escape from the sadness that seemed to characterize many aspects of her life. In the city, she was able to find a place to hide, to dream, to imagine; I've returned to those very gardens to do the same. I never did get to probe my parents with all of my questions about their reflections on urbanism that surely colored their views of the world. I miss them dearly. Mom and Dad, this book is dedicated to you.

Precarious Constructions

Introduction

> Multiculturalism is a fundamental characteristic of
> Canadian heritage and identity.
> —Canada, Multiculturalism Act, S.C. 1988 c. 31

A 2015 *Toronto Star* headline posed the question, "Sir John A. Macdonald: Nation Builder or Racist?"[1] Macdonald, Canada's first prime minister, is celebrated across Canada with statues, street names, and buildings honoring him as a founding father and symbol of Canadian national identity. Macdonald is well known for confederation, Canada's expansion, and the building of the Intercolonial and Pacific Railways.[2] He is also known for the creation of the Chinese Head Tax, the segregationist reserve system, brutal treatment of Indigenous peoples, and labeling those racialized as nonwhite as "savages" and lesser humans, if human at all.[3] For example, in one statement promoting residential schooling, Macdonald claimed that an Indigenous child educated in the child's own community "is simply a savage who can read and write," and asserted that those who attend residential schools "will acquire the habits and modes of thought of white men."[4] Macdonald suggested that integration might be possible through residential schooling—the violent removal of children from their families.

Why begin a book about public housing revitalization with reflections on the racism of Canada's first prime minister? This book challenges the assumption implicit in the newspaper headline that nation-building and racism are dichotomous in liberal democracies such as Canada. In fact, the construction of national identity goes hand in hand with racism despite claims of equality and acceptance promoted via Canadian neoliberal multiculturalism. *Precarious Constructions: Race, Class, and Urban Revitalization* examines two urban revitalization projects in Toronto, Regent Park and Lawrence Heights, as an entry point to explore broader questions about social regulation and the ways that racism, class hierarchy, and exclusion are foundational to liberal democracy in Canada. Although policy makers and urban planners often frame revitalization as a holistic approach that can resolve the segregation of public housing projects, this investigation provides insight into how the entanglement of multicultural and neoliberal values and ideals in revitalization

1

planning frameworks actually work against their stated efforts to promote integration. By looking more closely at the revitalization processes, I show how inequality becomes reproduced in obscure ways. A central claim of this book is that spatial (re)organization facilitated via urban revitalization creates and reproduces the very forms of difference that revitalization purports to manage.

The title, *Precarious Constructions*, signals my interest in multiple aspects of urban governance. The *Oxford English Dictionary* (2020) defines construction as:

1. The building of something, typically a large structure.
1.1 The building of large structures considered as an industry.
1.2 The style or method used in the building of something.
1.3 A building or other structure.
1.4 The creation or formation of an abstract entity.[5]

Construction can refer to the task of materially building something, as well as industry, building methods and aesthetics, and the material building itself. However, the term can also signal the construction of spaces and places, subjectivities, and the construction of our social worlds.[6] I investigate urban revitalization processes to consider the relationship between the built environment and urban populations and employ the term construction to interrogate the material and discursive building of public housing projects, neighborhoods and communities, race and class subjugation, and multiculturalism and national identity. I highlight the taken-for-granted nature of the building of spaces and subjectivities as constructions and as natural or neutral and examine how these constructions are both discursively and materially precarious.[7] Additionally, throughout the book, I emphasize processes of racialization and in some cases refer to Black, Indigenous, and people of color as "racialized as nonwhite." This language disrupts the ways that white supremacy benefits from whiteness's positioning as invisible, normative, or nonracialized.

I also employ the term construction in another sense. In each chapter I identify central planning tools—diversity, surveillance, and community consultations—that are used in the construction of the revitalization process in ways that both facilitate and legitimate revitalization. I argue that the deployment of these tools in the plans ultimately contributes to the (re)production of marginality for residents. By examining these tools, the many tensions and contradictions that emerge in their employment throughout the planning process shed light on the ways that addressing inequality in liberal democracies is never straightforward. These planning tools serve as social production *and* regulation technologies in urban planning that imply the integration of residents into rituals of democracy enmeshed with national ideals, but in fact depend on the (re)production and regulation of those marked as low-income and nonwhite public housing residents. I use the terms social (re)production and regulation to signal the disciplining of residents in relation to the built environment and revitalization process. In Foucauldian terms, "Discipline may be identified neither with an institution nor with an apparatus; it is a type of power, a modality for its exercise, comprising a whole set of instruments, techniques, procedures, levels of application, targets; it is a 'physics' or 'anatomy' of power, a technology."[8] Framing discipline as a technology and type of power allows us to explore how it operates as a tool for population management and social regulation. Inspired by this theorization, I understand diversity, surveillance, and consultations as interconnected disciplinary tools and technologies. By emphasizing the participation of culturally diverse, entrepreneurial subjects in community policing and community consultations, revitalization becomes a way to (re)produce and manage ethnoracial and class inequality. This book maps how these intertwined tools contribute to social management in cities by simultaneously *signaling* diversity, *normalizing* surveillance, and *mandating* community consultations. Diversity, surveillance, and consultations are framed as responses to address residential segregation but instead serve to (re)inscribe precarity and socioeconomic vulnerability for residents through various modes of engagement that limit possibilities for neighborhood transformation. More precisely, diversity is constructed as a celebration of culture, but on the ground, diversity requires disparity and obscures histories of racism; surveillance is constructed as a tool to create safety but is rooted in long histories of policing, exclusion, and stigmatization and encourages residents to criminalize one another; and consultations are constructed as strategies to promote resident engagement but in fact limit possibilities for participation. Diversity, surveillance, and consultations work together in the revitalization processes to reproduce race and class subjugation via neoliberal multiculturalism. For example, the emphasis on racial and economic diversity that I examine in chapter 2 legitimizes the need for increased surveillance in chapter 3. I show how, belying popular ideas about inclusiveness in Canada, the entanglement of neoliberalism and multiculturalism in urban revitalization reinscribes the very forms of difference (and inequality) it claims to manage and eradicate.

Central to my analysis is the careful consideration of residents' negotiation and contestation of their neighborhoods' remaking.

Each chapter of this book pursues an aspect of the entanglement of multiculturalism and neoliberalism, examining how urban revitalization projects become key sites for the construction, reproduction, and contestation of Canada's national identity as a model of inclusion in liberal democracies. The multicultural and neoliberal approaches infused in the revitalization process were employed in deceptive ways that hinge on the cachet of Canadian multiculturalism. Planning documents and comments at planning meetings and consultations frequently referenced multicultural and neoliberal values. For example, planning documents describe culture as a central planning concern, reference diversity as a value, or take note of residents' cultural differences, as well as their immigrant, newcomer, or citizenship status. Neoliberal values are embedded in a financial framework that is dependent on private developers and private investment to sustain revitalization. Neighborhood intensification is motivated by profit and market demands alongside limited public funding; Toronto Community Housing Corporation (TCHC) officials have asserted that a real estate market was created via the revitalization of public housing.[9] In addition to the "entrepreneurial" approach employed by TCHC, individual entrepreneurialism and business development are encouraged, and increased surveillance is promised to ensure economic regeneration and cultural diversity. These multicultural and neoliberal values are intertwined in planning discourses such as those suggesting that "the vibrant cultural mix and the young entrepreneurial demographic of Regent Park offer an opportunity to create a unique market or 'bazaar.'"[10] This statement signals the coupling of multiculturalism and neoliberalism by connecting cultural diversity to entrepreneurialism and individual success. Ultimately, the entanglement of multiculturalism and neoliberalism in revitalization serves to further entrench the logics of race and class hierarchy that are central to maintaining settler colonial capitalism in Canada.

The emphasis on diversity, surveillance, and consultations might seem natural and even progressive in the revitalization process; of course the urban revitalization should acknowledge and honor the populations that live in the neighborhoods, promote safety, and encourage resident participation in the design of their community. However, the positive valence of revitalization masks histories of structural inequality, residential segregation, and territorial stigmatization that cannot be addressed by invoking progressive ideals around inclusion. The many tensions and contradictions that emerge

Commission to address the questions of bilingualism and biculturalism given the presence of the "two founding" cultures in Canada, French and English.[25] The resulting policy, *Multiculturalism within a Bilingual Framework*, prescribed explicit acknowledgment of the variety of cultures in Canada, as well as the government's protection of rights for diverse cultural groups.[26] In the commission report, Indigenous peoples were not considered one of the two "founding races" or an immigrant or ethnic group, reflecting the settler colonial power relations that are tied to Canadian multiculturalism.[27] The multicultural national identity symbolized by a mosaic of cultures sharply contrasts with the US melting pot and a general understanding that the United States has a longstanding history of racism that is foundational to the country's character. Liberal positions on multiculturalism are frequently used to positively distinguish Canada from the United States.[28] As Political philospher Will Kymlicka argues, "Canada does better than virtually any other country in the world in the integration of immigrants."[29] Canadian "acceptance" and "tolerance" of different cultural groups and their traditions, embedded in Canadian law, often positions Canada as a model of liberal multiculturalism.

The Multiculturalism Act of 1988 expanded beyond French and English relations, including explicitly addressing the contributions and inclusion of immigrant communities. Further, it outlined the importance of eliminating racism and discrimination.[30] The act legally mandated *multiculturalism* to reinforce the idea that Canada welcomed and supported diversity and ethnic pluralism.

Liberal perspectives on multiculturalism in Canada promote the federal recognition of cultural differences. By liberal perspectives I am referring to the liberal political philosophical tradition, not simply progressive politics. My use of the term "liberal" aligns with Charles Mills's definition as an "antifeudal ideology of individualism, equal rights, and moral egalitarianism."[31] Liberal multiculturalism generally asserts that different cultural groups should not be discriminated against or excluded because of cultural practices (e.g., language, the celebration of religious holidays, etc.). Conservative critics of multiculturalism, on the other hand, question ideals around integration. Conservative perspectives both implicitly and explicitly express racist positions on immigration policy, as well as policies and practices that embrace different cultural and religious expressions. For example, Prime Minister Stephen Harper's (2002–2015) anti-immigrant tactics included asking Zunera Ishaq to remove her niqāb at a citizenship ceremony in 2013, jeopardizing her ability to become a citizen after years of waiting and passing the citizenship exam. This conservative backlash appears distinct from the liberal embrace of Canadian multiculturalism, as exemplified in mainstream Canadian media's praise of Prime Minister Justin Trudeau and Premier of Ontario Kathleen Wynne for greeting Syrian refugees at Toronto's Pearson Airport in 2015, suggesting that this illuminated the strengths of Canadian multiculturalism. Prime Minister Justin Trudeau, like his father Prime Minister Pierre Trudeau (1968–1979; 1980–1984), emphasized the centrality of multiculturalism and the value of cultural differences in the construction of Canadian identity. Justin Trudeau is often portrayed as a departure from the conservative Stephen Harper government that preceded Trudeau's tenure. Although Trudeau's promotion of Canadian multiculturalism appears to be incongruous to the racism of the Harper regime, celebrations of acceptance and diversity obscure historical fact.

While dominant liberal discourses describe multiculturalism and diversity as inherent strengths of Canadian national identity, by contrast, feminist and antiracist approaches provide a more critical view. Critics point to characterizations of Canadian multiculturalism as strategies for neutralizing power relations in the context of deepening divisions between groups along with and the promotion of superficial integration while neglecting power imbalances.[32] From this perspective, multicultural ideologies and political projects position diversity as a defining feature of Canadianness and an important political discourse. The rise of multiculturalism in Canada aligns with the denouncing of biological understandings of race that informed anti-Semitism and the persecution and genocide of Jewish peoples in World War II, as well as a distancing from various colonial-imperial racisms. A post–World War II shift to cultural framings of race and perceived human differences led to a rise of cultural diversity discourses that "redefines race as culture."[33]

Conservative, liberal, and critical perspectives yield much debate over the merit, purpose, and implementation of multiculturalism. The liberal perspectives of the 1990s emphasized the role of the policy of multiculturalism and its integrative features, while critical perspectives consider ideologies of multiculturalism in relation to histories of settler colonialism and racism.[34] Critiques of liberal multiculturalism have two main foci. The first is multiculturalism's superficial definition of culture, which it claims to celebrate. Critical scholars reference a symbolic model of multiculturalism that celebrates "saris, samosas and steel drums."[35] In this example, clothing, food, and music are the symbols of ethnic differences that can be consumed and celebrated in multicultural societies while often ignoring structural inequality and racism.

This is connected to a second area of criticism: that multiculturalism materially re-inscribes hierarchy and difference. Critical race and ethnic studies scholars have examined multiculturalism as it relates to the Canadian nation-building project by analyzing the role of the dominant "Canadian" (white) culture, the exclusion of Indigenous people, and the ways in which multiculturalism does not promote equality or equity among different cultural groups.[36] As Eva Mackey and Sunera Thobani argue, multicultural policy marks "other" cultures as "different," (re)producing white Canadians as the norm and establishing an ethnocultural hierarchy.[37] Multiculturalism presents race and culture as fixed, unchanging commodities to benefit the dominant culture.[38] Critical race and ethnic studies scholar Iyko Day poignantly asserts, "Canadian multiculturalism sidetracks race and class for a celebration of cultural difference."[39]

Multiculturalism is a "highly effective" way to manage difference because of its role as a federal policy, allowing the government to proclaim its ability to address cultural differences.[40] On a local level, questions of ethnic integration and multicultural cities preoccupy studies on urban life across borders. Dominant liberal discourses of multiculturalism generally describe urban communities as worthy of investment due to their cultural richness. This commodification of culture in cities points to the link between culture and urban spaces. Urban planners view some ethnic enclaves as assets to urban space, but only in relation to such commodified cultural elements as food and dance. In a post-9/11 context, multiculturalism and regulatory inclusion discourses were articulated alongside the policing and marginalization of different religious and ethnic groups. In this way, multiculturalism can be used to manage and subordinate urban populations, particularly low-income and nonwhite residents (chapter 3 explores the securitization of cities in relation to multiculturalism in detail).

Questions around pluralism and diversity, equity, and inclusion (DEI) have also been taken up in urban studies and planning. While nineteenth and early-to-mid-twentieth-century planning and urban studies, including the Atlanta School of Sociology and the Chicago School of Sociology, explored the integration, assimilation, and inequality of heterogeneous groups in cities, diversity has also been used to describe the built environment and desirable urban spaces. Jane Jacobs described diversity as the key feature of cities—meaning diversity of building types and uses as well as backgrounds and experiences.[41] Critical planning scholars have used theoretical and practical approaches to explore how diversity can remedy or address urban inequality.[42] In the contemporary moment, such approaches challenge neoliberal urban policies that further entrench segregation and urban poverty in the name of privatization and the free market.[43]

In relation to critical texts on the flexibility of the term "diversity," planning critiques are crucial for analyzing the ways in which diversity does not necessarily initiate social inclusion or the promotion of equity and access for "diverse" groups.[44] As planning scholar Susan Fainstein questions the assumption that there is a connection between "physical and social diversity." *Precarious Constructions* expands on these insights to explore the assumption that social diversity (culture and income) is linked to physical diversity (use and building types) alongside surveillance and consultations in Regent Park and Lawrence Heights. Additionally, *Precarious Constructions* draws from these interventions to examine how the logic of multiculturalism, while embracing a language of inclusion, integration, and acceptance, operates as a tool for social reproduction and regulation. In my investigation, I explore how multiculturalism became a "go-to," or normalized theme in the revitalization of Lawrence Heights and Regent Park because of multiculturalism's centrality to the construction of Canadian national identity. However, ideals around multiculturalism and the promotion of diversity were not mobilized in isolation from neoliberal governance; urban neoliberalism is also central to the multicultural logics employed to legitimize revitalization.

The Political Economy of Revitalization

Neoliberalism in Toronto has been explored at length in the context of urban development, urban policy, and housing.[45] Like multiculturalism, neoliberalism has a variety of manifestations and meanings. As a process, neoliberalism facilitates a simultaneous rollback or destruction of Keynesianism and a rollout of flows of capital to freely roam in global markets. Neoliberalism refers to the theory and practice of open markets and market-based solutions, or as geographer David Harvey describes, "deregulation, privatization, and withdrawal of the state from many areas of social provision."[46] As Neil Brenner and Nik Theodore write, "Neoliberalism powerfully structures the parameters for the governance of contemporary urban development—for instance, by defining the character of 'appropriate' policy choices, by constraining democratic participation in political life, by diffusing dissent and oppositional mobilization, and/or by disseminating new ideological visions of social and moral order in the city."[47] The diverse terrains that Brenner and Theodore identify reflect the profound structural effects of neoliberalism on urban life. While the extent of these effects is widely debated, urban scholars warn of neoliberalism's reach through urban governance.

The geographically contextual effects of neoliberalism have been theorized as "actually existing neoliberalism" or in the context of cities as "contingent urban neoliberalism."[48] Each of these perspectives insists upon the connection between local particularities and the everyday transformations neoliberalism enacts. As "contingent," urban neoliberalism takes shape differently, depending on context, and cannot be theorized as universal or unchanging.

Urban studies scholars have been particularly preoccupied with neoliberal policies in relation to processes of gentrification. Neoliberal policies facilitate the gentrification of urban neighborhoods following the logic of open markets through laissez-faire governance, the rolling back of the welfare state, public-private partnerships, and an emphasis on real estate investment.[49] Scholars often use the terms "gentrification" and "revitalization" interchangeably, although they are not necessarily the same. However, revitalization has been embraced as a term to describe state-managed gentrification.[50] Geographers Jason Hackworth and Neil Smith argue, "Gentrification has changed in ways that are related to larger economic and political restructuring. Among these changes is the return of heavy state intervention in the process."[51]

Ruth Glass coined the term "gentrification" in the 1960s to refer to the process (in London) by which lower income enclaves become upscale communities following the renovation and refurbishment of dwellings to meet the expectations of middle-class residents and the displacement of lower income residents.[52] Neil Smith examined gentrification in relation to the movement of capital and global economic restructuring.[53] Smith defined gentrification as "the process by which poor and working class neighborhoods in the inner city are refurbished via an influx of private capital and middle-class homebuyers and renters — neighborhoods that had previously experienced disinvestment and a middle-class exodus."[54] Elsewhere he summarizes gentrification as a process where "working class residential neighborhoods are rehabilitated by middle class homebuyers, landlords, and professional developers."[55] This perspective relies on an analysis of capitalism and class division whereby gentrification depends on the "movement of capital, not people," although evidence suggests they typically go hand in hand.[56] According to Kate Shaw, gentrification is the "generalized middle-class restructuring of place, encompassing the entire transformation from low-status neighborhoods to upper-middle-class playgrounds. Gentrifiers' residences are no longer just renovated houses but newly built townhouses

and high-rise apartments. . . . Gentrification extends to retail and commercial precincts, and can be seen in rural and coastal townships as well
as cities."[57]

To differentiate between early urban renewal schemes and gentrification,
Smith argues that post-war renewal schemes in the United States, which indeed facilitated "scattered private-market gentrification," combined with a
shift toward privatization in inner cities to establish the framework for the
gentrification of today.[58] These contemporary large-scale redevelopment
projects are now the norm in many cities—a far cry from sporadic "white-
painting" in the 1960s and 1970s.[59] Some view gentrification positively
because of increasing property values, reduced vacancy, and a return of
white populations to the city from suburban areas (reverse white flight).[60]
However, for low-income and racially stigmatized communities, gentrification, in fact, is a prime example of the effects of racial capitalism and its uneven impacts. These negative impacts include mass displacement, community
divisions, conflicts, and houselessness.[61] Neil Smith suggests that the language of regeneration "sugarcoats gentrification"; the term revitalization war-
rants a similar critique.[62] While I understand the revitalization of Regent
Park and Lawrence Heights as examples of gentrification, I use the term revitalization throughout *Precarious Constructions* to emphasize the particular
ways that revitalization becomes a legitimating neoliberal construction.

Finally, central to the entanglement between multiculturalism and neoliberalism is the settler colonial capitalist foundation on which urban revitalization hinges—I employ the word foundation in the literal sense of the
land as the foundation for the construction of buildings and the construction of Canada as a nation. Urban scholars have explored the branding and
marketing of redeveloped neighborhoods as a "frontier" to be conquered and
settled, framing gentrification as the new colonialism.[63] As both Clyde Woods
and Owen Toews have argued, this is not just metaphorical but rather evidence of the ongoing material nature of accumulation by dispossession.[64]
My analysis builds from critiques of settler colonial capitalist logics around
land and property that require the (attempted) extermination of Indigenous
peoples and the hypermanagement of potential laborers.[65] I understand the
framework of revitalization as an urban governance tool that contributes to
the maintenance of these logics and promotes gentrification.[66] As geographer Owen Toews asserts, "Capitalist struggles to remake cities, regions,
and countries, in other words, are processes where the contemporary character of settler colonialism—including the characters of race and state—is
renovated."[67] In urban revitalization projects, settler colonial capitalist log-

ics are articulated and legitimated via liberal discourses of integration. The intricate planning of revitalization operates in a broader context of settler colonial capitalism's flexibility and constant search for accumulation and profit, often employing liberal frameworks of multiculturalism, equity, and inclusion in ways that deceptively (re)produce cultural hegemony, inequity, and exclusion.

The Research

My qualitative multimethod approach incorporates analysis of planning documents, observations, and interviews. My document analysis includes planning documents from Lawrence Heights and Regent Park created between 2002 and 2015. My fieldwork took place between June 2010 and May 2011. I attended over one hundred hours of community and planning meetings, which allowed me to observe the various levels of organizing that shape the revitalization processes in both communities. During this time, I observed or participated in community meetings, consultations, community activities, and events in Regent Park and Lawrence Heights. In my fieldwork, I was able to draw on relationships that I formed from my work in the community as a tutor at the Regent Park Learning Center, where I taught English as a second language and reading to women from the community between 2009 and 2011. I attended meetings organized by the Lawrence Heights Inter-Organizational Alliance (LHION), BePART (a local resident participatory action group in Lawrence Heights), School Community Action Alliance Regent Park (SCAARP), the Social Development Plan (SDP) Stakeholders Table, TCHC consultations and meetings, and City of Toronto consultations and meetings. The community events I attended included the Regent Park Film Festival, where residents debated gentrification in Regent Park in relation to films screened at the festival; an antidevelopment rally in Lawrence Manor; and local vigils in response to community violence. I conducted semistructured interviews with twenty-one people who were connected to the revitalization projects in various capacities. Participants included four Lawrence Heights residents, one resident from Neptune, four Regent Park residents, one resident from Lawrence Manor, four City of Toronto planners, two representatives from the City of Toronto Revitalization Secretariat's Office, two community development liaisons from TCHC, and three community agency representatives. Engaging with residents, planners, and staff from community organizations allowed me to gain a better understanding of the many layers of the revitalization and consultation process, as well as stakeholders' and residents' varying perspectives on revitalization, community, and belonging. Pseudonyms are used for all interviewees to protect their anonymity.

Chapter Map

In chapter 1, "Neighborhood and Nation: Constructing Public Housing," I explore histories of revitalization in Lawrence Heights and Regent Park as microcosms of the broader history of housing policy in Canada. In particular, I focus on key moments in housing policy at the local, provincial, and federal levels, as well as the transition from the welfare state to neoliberal governance. Exploring these connections is central to understanding how and why urban revitalization projects are such meaningful contexts for investigating questions around social, political, and economic inclusion and exclusion in liberal democracies. The historical framework in this chapter provides a backdrop for chapters 2, 3, and 4, where I examine how diversity, surveillance, and participation are mobilized in the revitalization processes to signal inclusion and belonging but in fact require and reproduce race and class inequality.

Chapter 2, "Precarious Mosaic: Diversity or Disparity in Toronto's Regent Park?" engages with recent debates in Canada about the role of cultural diversity in the changing urban landscape and the impact of neoliberalism and economic reinvestment in urban development.[68] Central to my argument is challenging the framing of diversity as emerging from bodies and demographics, and instead reconceptualizing diversity as produced through modes of governance. I zoom in on the Regent Park revitalization plans to explore how the use of diversity simultaneously aligns with neoliberal discourses and, more traditionally, with multiculturalism. I analyze the emphasis on three types of diversity that shape the Regent Park revitalization: diversity of use, diversity of income, and diversity of culture. I argue that the *diversity of diversities* serves as a legitimating tool for the revitalization project and hinges on the cachet of Canadian multiculturalism. The main tensions that emerge in chapter 2 are around how urban revitalization can acknowledge the histories of cultural diversity in the neighborhood without framing diversity as an aspect of the neighborhood that needs to be fixed or addressed in the process.

In chapter 3, "Neoliberal Surveillance and Eyes on the Street,'" I explore how the seemingly progressive use of diversity in revitalization (chapter 2) becomes intertwined with surveillance and the logic of the security state. I expand my analysis to include both Lawrence Heights and Regent Park to explore how the planning documents emphasize the incorporation of policing and surveillance in the urban design and architecture of the new development. The *Regent Park Revitalization Study* and planning documents actually call on residents to patrol one another; the study speculates that the revitalization will "improve safety through more 'eyes on the street' and provide opportunities for the community to celebrate and share its diverse cultures. It would provide spaces for economic regeneration, educational programs, community gardens, recreational activities and arts and cultural programs."[69] This passage portrays participation in community policing as a means by which residents can celebrate multiculturalism, which is linked to increased opportunities for the economic regeneration of the community. In chapter 3 I argue that "eyes on the street" produces two types of surveillance in Regent Park and Lawrence Heights: normalizing surveillance and negotiated surveillance. Normalizing surveillance refers to the ways that the revitalization process promoted and encouraged participation in neighbor-to-neighbor policing as the common sense way to build community and to make the neighborhood safe and integrated with the surrounding social fabric. In this contradictory logic, surveillance is a key method of producing a unified community, yet residents are recruited to distinguish between and police one another based on granular scales of perceived criminality. Negotiated surveillance, on the other hand, references the ways that residents make sense of surveillance and policing. One key tension that emerges in the employment of eyes on the street and community policing is how to promote safety under neoliberal multiculturalism without surveillance and racial profiling.

While chapter 3 examines participation in surveillance, chapter 4, "Canadians in the Making: Community Engagement and Procedural Participation," explores participation in the revitalization consultation process. In chapter 4 I trace how revitalization recruited residents to participate in consultations and simultaneously limited their participation. I investigate how the City of Toronto and TCHC constructed consultation as a technology that prescribed and limited the nature of participation despite claims that consultations would create belonging for public housing residents. TCHC and the City of Toronto positioned consultations as an inherent feature of the revitalization and a reflection of the importance of democratic engagement — especially for new immigrants or newcomers.[70] Planners described participation as a tool to teach "Canadianness" to residents. However, residents understood their participation in more nuanced ways. I explore the role of what I label neoliberal "procedural participation" that generically positioned participation as an instrumentalist opportunity to teach residents the legitimate habits of political engagement. Although procedural participation utilized the language of inclusion and engagement, it did so in ways that ultimately limited residents' participation.

Collectively, the chapters of *Precarious Constructions* demonstrate that revitalization processes systematically and deceptively project the appearance of inclusion while reproducing social inequality. Urban revitalization projects, in other words, are framed as a response to the preexisting problems public housing presents in a seemingly progressive multicultural society (e.g., segregation, income disparity, and lack of access to resources). However, these projects become key sites for the strategic production and maintenance of socioeconomic precarity despite institutional claims of neutrality. While diversity is positioned as something to celebrate and honor, diversity hinges on disparity. The selective and legitimating use of diversity is (re)produced and managed via surveillance and political participation. Signaling diversity, safety, and community participation in urban revitalization may promote normative liberal ideas around Canadian national identity, yet they re-entrench neoliberal multiculturalism and ultimately attempt to naturalize forms of difference and inequality, ignoring the histories of settler colonial capitalism in Canada that are the very foundation on which such processes are discursively and materially built.

Precarious Constructions

A 2016 *New York Times* article featured Toronto's Regent Park as a model for urban revitalization: "In Toronto, a Neighborhood of Despair Transforms into a Model of Inclusion." That the *New York Times* would feature a story in Section A of the print edition about a Toronto neighborhood is noteworthy, but it is perhaps unsurprising that the article highlights inclusion, cultural diversity, and multiculturalism. Canada is well known for its approach to multiculturalism and touts its mosaic brand in opposition to the assimilationist or melting-pot approach of the United States. As a multicultural mosaic, Canada purports to include, honor, and celebrate people from different cultural, racial, and ethnic backgrounds, whereas the melting-pot approach in the United States aims to absorb or assimilate different groups into Anglo-American culture and identity. The article praises the efforts toward inclusion: "As Canada accepts 25,000 Syrian refugees, the new Regent Park, thick with immigrants from Africa, Asia and the Caribbean, provides a blueprint for successful economic and cultural integration."[71] As a blueprint, the article praises the revitalization's successful integration of its immigrant population.

While Canada is recognized for multiculturalism, especially in contrast to its neighbor to the south, such celebrations obscure the histories and impacts of structural racism. To take one example, Canada remains a settler colonial nation, and its Indigenous communities continue to experience systemic exclusion, segregation, hyperpolicing, violence, and everyday hardship. Critics emphasize that multicultural policy often frames Indigenous populations as another ethnic group, ignoring their sui generis rights.[72] Canada's identity as a beacon of inclusion and equality is therefore precarious, at best.

As Nandita Sharma writes, "Home, and the ways it helps to organize ideas of family, household ethnic community, and nation, is one of the most naturalized concepts and therefore one of the most dangerous. Modernist ideas of home, in particular, help to organize and legitimate the differential treatment of those living within the same space. Differences between diverse indigenous people, citizens, immigrants, and migrant workers are organized through ideas of Canada being the home of some but not to others."[73] *Precarious Constructions* draws links between the micro scale of the construction of housing and homes in cities to the macro scale of the construction of homeland and national identity. Looking closely at the revitalization of two public housing projects in Toronto, I examine how efforts to integrate immigrants, "culturally diverse groups," and segregated neighborhoods actually (re)produce ethnoracial and class hierarchies. I argue that although urban revitalization purports to address socioeconomic segregation, neoliberal multicultural revitalization produces and reproduces the very forms of racial and class hierarchy it claims to manage. While this book focuses on the construction of two particular neighborhoods in a single city, the ubiquity of institutional discourses that promote diversity, protests about racial profiling and policing, and ruptures in political participation have broad implications for understanding the often obscure and discrete ways neoliberal inequality is reproduced across societal scales and national borders.

CHAPTER ONE

Neighborhood and Nation

Constructing Public Housing

> Housing is such a bedrock of society—Canada is not a country to be lived in without shelter—that its influences permeate all aspects of social and economic life.
>
> —JOHN SEWELL (Former Mayor of Toronto), *Housing and Homes*, 1994, 4

> The residential is political—which is to say that the shape of the housing system is always the outcome of struggles between different groups and classes. Housing necessarily raises questions about state action and the broader economic system.
>
> —DAVID MADDEN AND PETER MARCUSE, *In Defense of Housing*, 2016, 4

Liberal rights discourses frame housing outcomes as a result of individual choices and bootstrap mythologies. Those who work hard will have ample access to resources and housing options. However, a closer look at the history of housing policies tells a different story. As Madden and Marcuse argue, "The residential is political."[1] The residential is political because where one lives is connected to affordability, generational wealth, histories of segregation, employment opportunities, education, and more.

This chapter sheds light on often taken for granted aspects of housing policy to center housing as a key site to examine and understand national priorities, political commitments, and values. Building on historian Sean Purdy's assertion that housing policy becomes an essential space for the making of citizens and laborers, I trace the connection between the rescaling of the welfare state and public housing redevelopment via revitalization (or neoliberal state-managed gentrification).[2] I situate the original planning and construction of Regent Park and Lawrence Heights in the context of the rise of the welfare state in Canada and provide a selective overview of the subsequent neoliberal turn in housing policy and revitalization. I explore key moments in Canadian housing policy at the federal, provincial, and local levels between the 1940s and 2000s, with particular focus on the City of Toronto, and trace the connections between Keynesian and neoliberal urban revitalization.

The City of Toronto

To offer a brief geographical introduction (more expansive historical and demographic details are provided throughout chapter 1), Toronto is located in the Province of Ontario. It is Canada's largest city and the fourth largest city in North America. It is considered one of the most ethnoracially diverse cities in North America, with a population of approximately 3 million. The City of Toronto is located on traditional territory of Mississaugas of the Credit, the Anishnabeg, the Chippewa, the Haudenosaunee, and the Wendat peoples. Toronto is located approximately eighty miles north of Niagara Falls and sits next to Lake Ontario, with the New York State border just to the south.

Urban Renewal in Canada

Regent Park and Lawrence Heights were constructed in response to a housing shortage and lack of affordable housing in the late 1940s and 1950s. In 1934, the *Bruce Report* was published and examined housing conditions in Toronto under the auspices of the lieutenant governor. Surveying over 1,300 dwellings, the report revealed shocking cases of inadequate living conditions around the city.[3] It described the area now known as Regent Park as an example of the lowest standard of living in the City of Toronto.[4] The city used the report to solicit publicly funded housing for the city's lower-income populations.

The ten years following the publication of the *Bruce Report* saw a flurry of provincial and federal plans, reports, commissions, and conferences on housing. In turn, there was much debate over developing a federal housing plan that would reshape housing for Canadians and affect loans, mortgages, and subsidized housing units. These debates eventually led to the passing of laws that would pave the way for new housing legislation in Canada. At the same time, multiple local and national initiatives specifically focused on redevelopment and renewal.

The terms revitalization and urban renewal began popping up all over cities in the United States and Canada in the 1930s and 1940s, respectively. Despite many differences between housing policies in the United States and Canada, several similar trends emerged because of overlapping economic and historical events (including World War II and the shift to a rise of neoliberalism in the 1980s, for example). Urban renewal in Canada and the United States focused on "run-down" residential neighborhoods in cities or on land that was needed to develop infrastructure (e.g., highways); renewal programs centered on physical change in urban areas.[5] Canada addressed the problem of slums and declining conditions in cities through the Dominion Housing Act of 1935, the National Housing Act of 1944 (and subsequent amendments), and more explicitly in the creation of the Urban Renewal Program that aimed to "improve deteriorating areas of cities."[6] Similar to the United States, the Canadian government framed housing as a national concern. Renewal, in particular, prioritized neighborhoods that housed the "urban poor" under the logic of the welfare state.

Renewal efforts targeted whole neighborhoods as a way to bring transformation to areas of cities that were deemed "blighted." While the histories of renewal in the United States and Canada differ, under urban renewal, many low-income neighborhoods were completely torn down. In some cases, this occurred legally through eminent domain and expropriation, respectively, which gave local governments full power to remove residents with no guarantee of return. "Slum" areas inhabited by low-income residents living in dilapidated housing were bulldozed to make way for new housing, commercial buildings, or public infrastructure. New housing often took the form of public housing buildings, like those in Regent Park and Lawrence Heights.

Regent Park and Lawrence Heights: 1940–1980

Regent Park

Regent Park, Toronto's oldest and largest public housing community, was built between 1947 and 1958. In the broader Canadian and North American context that shaped its construction, post–World War II slum clearance policies encouraged tearing down housing in lower-income neighborhoods and replacing them with publicly funded housing. Born out of slum clearance, Regent Park was built as part of the Federal Urban Renewal Program and was considered an "experiment" in public housing in Canada. Prior to the construction of the public housing project, the neighborhood was considered one of the worst areas in the city. It was notorious not only for crime, violence, and poverty, but also for the smell of cabbages that residents grew in their front yards.

Regent Park is located just west of Toronto's Don Valley Parkway (the parkway was built between 1958 and 1966), one of the city's main highways. The housing complex is bordered by Gerrard Street to the north, Parliament Street to the west, Queen Street to the south, and River Street to the east. It is just one block south of Toronto's well-known Victorian-style, gentrified neighborhood, Cabbagetown.[7] Regent Park is also in close proximity to Toronto's lakeshore and financial and shopping districts.

Regent Park North, the northern and older section of today's Regent Park, was the first official large-scale public housing project in Toronto. The passage of City of Toronto bylaw no. 17080 in 1947 made its construction possible.[8] In spite of some voters' hostility and opposition toward housing for those with lower incomes, the ratepayers of Toronto voted for the $6 million project in a local referendum in 1946.[9] While priority was given to former Cabbagetown residents who lived on the land where the new housing was built, the project would also provide temporary housing for returning World War II veterans and low-to-middle-income residents in the area. Regent Park North welcomed its first residents in 1948.

In the 1950s, the city expanded the neighborhood with the construction of Regent Park South. Consisting of thirty residential buildings, by 2004 the neighborhood would come to house approximately 7,500 residents. Early residents were primarily of Irish and English descent. It spanned two superblocks and consisted of both townhouses and apartment style high-rise structures and covered sixty-nine acres. The 2,083 units included studio, one, two, three, four, and five-bedroom units. While the early design of Regent Park North followed a garden city design model, Regent Park South was inspired by Le Corbusier's modernist urban architectural vision that informed the planning of many high-rise public housing projects across North America and Europe. Although the design of the neighborhood was often praised in its early days, it would become critiqued by residents, planners, and scholars as a design that facilitated the segregation of urban lower-income populations because its inward facing buildings and lack of through streets separated it from the surrounding neighborhoods, a design that became characteristic of public housing in the United States and Canada.

In the postwar period, the construction of public housing in Canada was based on the premise that residents would live there temporarily and then move into the private market with the support of homeownership programs. They were therefore designed not to compete with private-market units, either visually or in terms of quality.[10] The *Toronto Star* nonetheless described Regent Park in 1950 as "heaven," emphasizing the presence of veterans.[11] A member of the city government gestured to the national valence of the project in 1949 when he said the complex should have a sign proclaiming "Good Citizens Dwell Here."[12] Public officials argued the new developments would rejuvenate the city's tax base and support the service-based economy by providing housing for the local workforce.[13]

Initially heralded as a success and model for the construction of other low-income or public housing communities, by the mid-1950s newspapers described Regent Park as a planning failure, a "ghetto" housing a "poor" population, with high levels of crime and violence and isolation from other Toronto neighborhoods.[14] A city planner called public housing a "giveaway" in the *Globe and Mail* in 1956. The article described Regent Park housing as notorious and wrote that it was designed in the "wrong place, for the wrong people [and built] in an erratic, unplanned manner which cannot stand up to reasonable examination."[15]

In 1968 the Ontario Housing Corporation, the provincial housing agency, took over the management of Regent Park from the Toronto Housing Authority (THA). The province contracted the Metro Toronto Housing Authority (MTHA) to manage Regent Park. The MTHA was far less present than the THA had been, as it was responsible for the entire metropolitan area, and it imposed a new administrative structure that lowered the standard of living in the neighborhood. Asking management to address everyday problems with plumbing or maintenance required extensive bureaucratic procedures.

A 1972 report on Regent Park North by the Toronto Development Department Research and Information Division painted a different picture of the complex. Titled *Canada's Premier Housing Redevelopment Project*, it compared conditions in Regent Park North after redevelopment with those that had prevailed in the same space in the 1930s and 1940s. It highlighted increased green space and a decrease in arrests.[16] The report touted improved well-being and overall health, especially for children. These reports shed light on the fact that, although there were problems with the design of Regent Park, there were also aspects that improved some facets of resident life, especially the formation of a strong sense of community among many tenants.

Nonetheless, by 2002, when the Regent Park Collaborative Team published its study on the revitalization project, rehabilitating and revitalizing Regent Park was thought to be the best way forward by the city, housing authorities, and several community organizations.[17] Ongoing debates over "what to do with Regent?" throughout its history had ceded to agreement among planners, however the particular process and plan would lead to much disagreement among residents and onlookers.[18] In many accounts, revitalization was the natural next step because of the outdated design—obsolescence was a central justification to help support what was constructed as the natural evolution to bring Regent Park into the twenty-first century.

Lawrence Heights

The development of the Lawrence Heights public housing project began in 1955. The land that is now home to Lawrence Heights originally belonged to the Mulholland family farm. After the Canadian Mortgage and Housing Company (CMHC) bought the land, it would become a site to test the new federal-provincial partnership on housing managed by the CMHC. The CMHC developed single-family homes in the area during the 1940s in response to the postwar housing shortage.[19] The CMHC worked with metropolitan Toronto "to build social housing on the area's remaining land—the beginnings of the Lawrence Heights Neighborhood."[20] The Township of North York was located approximately ten kilometers north of downtown Toronto. Unlike Regent Park, Lawrence Heights faced significant resistance from the local community of North York, which deemed it a threat to traditional rural ways of life (North York became part of the Greater Toronto Area in the amalgamation of surrounding regions to the City of Toronto in 2000).[21] Housing projects of this kind were generally located in cities, where they did not have as large an effect on population density. In posing their objections, the North York Township argued that an increase of low-income families would require more social services in the area that would strain local budgets.[22] However, Albert Rose's documentation on Lawrence Heights and concerns around impacts on rural ways of life signal broader concerns about the class stigma already attached to public housing projects such as Regent Park.

Despite the resistance of local residents, CMHC completed Lawrence Heights by 1959 and sited the agency headquarters within the complex. According to the city's revitalization plan, upon completion of construction, Lawrence Heights was "greeted with enthusiasm by the public."[23] The design was based on the garden city model and spanned on 60½ hectares of land.[24] Designers used Regent Park as a model for Lawrence Heights, and like Regent Park, it was designed with inward facing buildings that effectively isolated the community from surrounding neighborhoods.

Lawrence Heights is surrounded by Lawrence Avenue to the south, Ranee Avenue to the north, Varna Drive and Cather Crescent to the east, Flemington Road to the west, and straddles both sides of Allen Road (colloquially called "the Allen"), one of the city's main highways.[25] Prior to revitalization, Toronto Community Housing Corporation (TCHC) owned and operated 1,208 subsidized units and it was home to approximately 3,500 residents.[26]

Before revitalization, the housing project consisted of two, three, and four-story walk-up apartment buildings and townhouses. While the streets were designed to discourage traffic congestion by blocking the neighborhood off from surrounding areas, just as Regent Park had been, it was considerably less dense than Regent Park. Building heights were determined in part to accommodate the needs of pilots landing planes at nearby Downsview Airport, as taller buildings would have obstructed views.[27]

In keeping with the garden city planning style, Lawrence Heights was designed around a central green space, Flemington Park. However, Allen Road was built running through the neighborhood. Local activists, with the assistance of the famous urbanist, author, and journalist Jane Jacobs, challenged the siting of the expressway, to no avail. The Allen runs directly through the neighborhood and makes traveling from one side of the neighborhood to the other difficult as one has to walk to Lawrence Avenue, Flemington Road, or Ranee Avenue.

Racial Spatial Segregation in Regent Park and Lawrence Heights

The building of Regent Park and Lawrence Heights in the 1940s and 1950s should be examined in relation to the social and political context, specifically as it relates to race and class segregation. As Stefan Kipfer and Jason Petrunia note, the development of public housing cannot be detached from processes of racialization and racism: "Racialization and racism are intrinsic to the formation, crisis, and delegitimization of public housing."[28] In fact, the postwar model of functionally separating and hierarchically ordering urban space was most acute in the planning of public housing projects. This was particularly the case where public housing was always strongly residual and housed non-European residents from the beginning (in the United States and, more selectively, Canada).[29]

The designs of Regent Park and Lawrence Heights are no exception and emulate the functional separation and ordering of urban space that Kipfer and Petrunia critique.[30] In fact, the deterioration of the housing stock that resulted from postwar planning practices easily became tied to the pathology of residents racialized as nonwhite. While early residents in both neighborhoods were primarily racialized as white, they were marked by their low-income class status. In relation to Regent Park, Sean Purdy suggests, "The powerful demonization of Regent Park as a site of social depravity and behavioral deficiency became a central feature of tenants' lives in the country's largest housing project."[31] While Lawrence Heights and Regent Park are unique given their distinct histories and spatial organization, the stigma attached to both is connected to a broader history of racial spatial segregation and the constructed pathology associated with public housing in the mid-twentieth century.

While many public housing projects in Canada in the 1940s, 1950s, and 1960s were predominantly Euro-Canadian neighborhoods, African, Caribbean, Latin American, Asian, and South Asian communities would begin to increasingly populate public housing beginning in the 1970s. Canada experienced an influx of immigrants in the 1960s and 1970s to address a labor shortage. Changes to racist and exclusionary immigration policies and factors including war, decolonization, and political upheavals emerged alongside the official implementation of Canadian multiculturalism. As such, Regent Park and Lawrence Heights became associated with ethnoracial, low-income immigrant populations, and the public increasingly blamed these populations for the physical degradation of public housing projects.

In Toronto and Ontario more broadly, many community organizations fought for affordable housing options. Community leaders and community organizations paved the way for public housing to be accepted by local and federal governments. Veterans' and women's groups joined struggles for adequate housing after World War II and experienced significant wins with the creation of thousands of units. Social struggles continued into the 1970s and 1980s in Toronto, during which time social housing units made up 20 percent of new rental units. Many contemporary local and provincial community groups including neighborhood health centers, the Ontario Coalition Against Poverty, Ontario's Advocacy Centre for Tenants, and CivicAction carry on the work of housing and social justice advocates who fought to raise awareness and change policy at Toronto City Hall. Various social justice efforts challenged the ideological shifts from the 1980s onward, when housing was taken off social policy agendas and left to the private market, abdicating the state from taking responsibility and providing basic social support for residents.

Ultimately, the 1970s and 1980s were a period of ramping up of processes of gentrification.[32] But this shift is part and parcel of a broader set of processes of renewal and revitalization. Some urban redevelopment schemes, such as those in Africville in Halifax and Chinatown in Vancouver, were clearly articulated as strategies of revitalizing spaces racialized as nonwhite.[33] Earlier welfare state and social supports allowed white residents to move out of public housing into the private real estate market as renters or homeowners, and nonwhite immigrants (following Pierre Trudeau's liberalization of immigration policy in the late 1960s) moved in during a period of intense deindustrialization, urban disinvestment, and a diminishing welfare state. As a result of the changing populations and socioeconomic climate, the dynamics of territorial stigmatization had shifted, which lay the groundwork for more redevelopment.[34] Public housing developments ultimately became the signature image of "racialized urban space."[35] While the urban renewal of the late 1940s and early 1950s in Canada was designed to address housing issues for primarily white, urban, poor residents and returning veterans and was supported by welfare state policies, in the ensuing decades revitalization intersected with the rise of neoliberal multiculturalism.

Neoliberal Toronto and the Revitalization of Regent Park and Lawrence Heights

The revitalization of Regent Park and Lawrence Heights in the 2000s is tied to a long history of shifting philosophies about public housing and redevelopment. Specifically, with a rescaling of the welfare state, a new phase of revitalization has emerged in which public housing redevelopment is delivered via state-managed gentrification. This rescaling involves changes from previous legislation that promoted and enabled the allocation of public resources to housing as well as a transformation of the administration of public housing whereby it operates as a quasi-private business enterprise; it involves the deregulation of housing that is central to the contemporary logic of "revitalization." The idea that public housing was a temporary solution, a stepping stone to homeownership in the commodified housing market, makes its dismantling politically palatable. Further, a lack of government funding for public housing legitimizes neoliberal approaches to revitalization that sell public lands to the private sector. One key distinction from neighborhood revitalization in the United States is that with exception of the Neighborhood Improvement Program in the 1970s, there were limited policies or resources across the three levels of government to address the inadequate housing conditions and segregation of neighborhoods like Regent Park and Lawrence Heights. While urban revitalization in the 1980s was focused on federal fiscal restraint and promoting "sporadic" gentrification and downtown development, urban revitalization in the 1990s and 2000s mobilized a rhetoric of holistic place-based strategies that stood in contrast to the failed approaches of the twentieth century.

Contemporary revitalization schemes in Toronto emerged in relation to changes in social housing policy in Canada in the 1990s.[36] The federal conservative Mulroney government of the early 1980s initiated budget cuts and reorganized federal-provincial housing relations.[37] In the 1990s the federal government took social housing off the agenda.[38] It offloaded responsibility to provinces at a time when federal funding was the main source for local service providers. By 1993, federal funding for new housing units was almost nonexistent.[39] In 1993, the federal government declared that there would be no new commitments to social housing in Canada. With the exception of support for housing on reservations for Indigenous communities, the Canadian government solidified the expiry of federal pledges for social housing.

Following federal shifts in policy, in 1995 the Harris government in Ontario transformed housing policy and governance in the province. Harris's stated aim was to get Ontario "out of the housing business."[40] He cut provincial funding for social housing and the province off-loaded $905 million in social housing costs to the municipalities, making them responsible for all housing complexes the province had previously managed.

The Social Housing Reform Act (SHRA) "formalized" the restructuring in 2000.[41] The main goal of this act was to ensure that housing providers forged relationships with private investors and the private market. As such, housing providers were expected to function as businesses, turning profit and paying taxes.[42] The provincial government not only encouraged deregulation but also encouraged housing providers to be entrepreneurial, partnering with and functioning like the developers and landlords in the private housing market.[43]

The downloading of administration of social housing to municipalities, regulated through the SHRA, meant that local property taxes would cover social housing as opposed to government assistance; this is a dramatic shift, as the federal government previously provided 75 percent of funding. Further, housing providers were given more responsibility with less autonomy.[44] Providers had to operate in an environment of increased "bureaucratic hurdles" and were expected to navigate a more centralized housing system.[45] Thus, paradoxically, even as the responsibilities of providing housing moved to the local level, housing became more centralized, as opposed to less, because of management and administrative issues.

For example, as a result of provincial downloading, the City of Toronto administers public housing with little to no aid from the province or federal government. Neoliberal restructuring had severe effects on the city's ability to maintain housing, which put thousands of housing units at risk of being sold to the private market. A transformation of public housing to a quasi-private economic enterprise reorganized government control. While neoliberal restructuring promised to address a crisis in social housing using the language of the free market, it continues to be deficient in its ability to provide access to opportunities for all residents.

The neoliberal shifts in policy in the 1990s and 2000s are often erroneously described as state withdrawal from housing policy, but administrative structures were centralized, and housing providers' responsibility increased while having less autonomy.[46] Under urban neoliberal governance, the state does not absolve itself of responsibility from social services such as public housing; instead, the nature and structure of state intervention shifts. This rearticulation of state intervention increasingly aligns housing policy with the logics of capitalism and the commodification of housing. In this context, neoliberal urban revitalization becomes the solution to addressing the constructed crisis of public housing. At the local level, urban revitalization emerged as the go-to framework and was framed as a problem of obsolescence to deal with the state's failures and lack of commitment to provide affordable housing.

In Toronto, as a result of the SHRA changes, the city oversees all social housing providers. TCHC was created in 2002 from the merging of City Home, Toronto Metropolitan Housing Corporation, and the Toronto Housing Company. Officials touted the merging as a way to make the management of housing easier and more accessible to tenants, although researchers suggest it actually increased bureaucratic hurdles and waiting lists.[47] TCHC is the largest public housing organization in Canada and provides affordable housing to approximately 165,000 tenants across 60,000 units in over 2,100 buildings. It is the second largest housing provider in North America, next to the New York City Housing Authority. TCHC's mandate is "to provide clean, safe, secure homes in a state of good repair to low and moderate-income households, including seniors, families, singles, refugees, recent immigrants to Canada, and people with special needs."[48] Their responsibilities include developing and facilitating the development of affordable and subsidized rental housing; delivering program related services and supporting other organizations to provide tenant related services and programs; developing and operating commercial spaces and services that support TCHC, and operating subsidized rental housing.[49] TCHC has been the subject of numerous scandals, and housing shortages remain even as a crisis with maintaining and repairing units has developed.[50] Neoliberal urban revitalization frameworks were first introduced in Toronto in the late 1990s. Rivertowne, formerly known as Don Mount Court, located in Toronto's east end, was the first mixed-income redevelopment project in Canada and began in 2002. The revitalization of Regent Park would become the first large-scale revitalization, beginning in 2005. By 2017, ten TCHC neighborhoods were undergoing revitalization. However, as political scientists Horak and

Moore highlight, the impact of neighborhood revitalization is limited because there has not been broader institutional change that can support revitalization as an impactful or lasting social policy.[51] Reflecting on revitalization in Toronto, they argue, "Instead, the preexisting institutional system has remained intact, and its features have in turn shaped and constrained neighborhood revitalization policies. These institutional features include the insulation of neighborhood social concerns from ward-based political representation, the absences of an overarching coordinating authority for place-based social intervention, and the limited, fragmented, and short-term availability of financing for neighborhood revitalization. Under these structural conditions, Toronto's policymakers have been able to implement revitalization as planned only in instances where they have chosen to harness the forces of the real estate market in pursuit of physical reconstruction."[52] Under the neoliberal financial framework to redevelop public housing in Ontario, the private sector is responsible for redeveloping the land and selling pieces of it (including condos). TCHC's financial framework is described as "leveraging social housing" in order to rebuild the housing stock. In the case of Regent Park and Lawrence Heights, public-private partnerships generate revenue for basic maintenance, repair, and related issues. As urban scholar Faranak Miraftab argues, public-private partnerships are the "Trojan horse of neoliberalism" because they obscure power relations between the different stakeholders.[53] The revitalization financial frameworks rely on the privatization of the land and selling market-value units to generate revenue to redevelop public housing. In short, urban revitalization is fundamentally neoliberal in character. Because of a lack of federal and provincial funding and provision support, the revitalization of public housing depends on private investment where public lands are sold to the private sector. The lack of funding and support is reflected in the Province of Ontario's and the city's limited budgets for affordable housing. For example, from 2014 to 2019, the provincial government spent "less than .3 percent of their total budgets on housing programs."[54] The projections from 2019 to 2028 estimate that the provincial contributions will continue to decrease by approximately $150 million per year.[55] Under these conditions, the city and housing providers are left to develop solutions to provide affordable housing.

The Revitalization of Regent Park

The Regent Park revitalization began in 2005 and was estimated to take 20–25 years to complete construction.[56] Before revitalization, Regent Park consisted of 2,083 rent-geared-to-income (RGI) units with approximately 7,500 residents. According to the 2006 census (the last census before large-scale relocation), 80 percent of the population of Regent Park identified as visible minorities (higher than the Toronto average of 50 percent), with a large population of South Asian, Black, and Chinese residents. Sixty percent of residents identified as immigrants. The median income was approximately $24,775, below the low-income cutoff (in 2006 the low-income cutoff was $27,745 for a family of four).[57]

TCHC's 2004 Annual Review announced that "after decades of need and many unsuccessful attempts, renewal is finally coming to Regent Park," referencing a long-standing desire on behalf of residents and planners to address the deteriorating housing stock.[58] TCHC described Regent Park as in "need of massive capital investment in buildings, improved neighborhood design and integration with surrounding communities."[59] Upon completion, there will be 1,817 RGI units in Regent Park with 266 replaced in new buildings nearby. (This is a point of contention for residents that I highlight in chapter 2. Originally, revitalization promised to replace all social housing units on the footprint of Regent Park.) RGI housing units regulate the rent in relation to residents' income, where generally, households pay approximately 30 percent of their gross income toward their rent.[60]

The TCHC *Report on the Regent Park Revitalization Study* promises revitalization will create a "more typical Toronto neighborhood."[61] The documents critique the brick and mortar approach that characterized the original construction plan for the neighborhood, which only focused on the material building structures as opposed to incorporating social and commercial development in the neighborhood.[62] The *Revitalization Study* promises to connect the "replanned and redeveloped neighborhood seamlessly with surrounding neighborhoods."[63] To wit, it claims revitalization will bring vitality to the community by providing housing, businesses, education, recreation, green spaces, transportation, and community services.

The 2004 TCHC annual review claimed that "when the plan is put into action it will help in the effort to create a healthy, strong and vital community."[64] This echoed the claims of the 2002 study that declared the buildings in Regent Park had "become dysfunctional" because they "increased the sense of isolation in the neighborhood and created spaces for crime and vandalism" even though they were "structurally sound."[65] Documents generated from 2002 to 2004 describe Regent Park's isolation from Cabbagetown and Corktown, its neighboring gentrified communities. The promise of revitalization was that its holistic approach would provide economic opportunities to Regent Park's disenfranchised residents by ending segregation.

Regent Park is being revitalized to become a mixed-use and mixed-income neighborhood. A mixed-use framework addresses the lack of commercial, recreational, and community spaces in the neighborhoods (as opposed to single-use residential zoning used in its original construction), while a mix of incomes and tenures is meant to address the concentration of low-income people in public housing. Mixed-income and tenure refers to the combination of private-market units and subsidized RGI public housing units. A mix of tenures, tied to the mix of incomes, refers to the private market (owned) and both affordable and subsidized rental units. While the plan celebrated the proposed mixed-use framework and introduction of community spaces and social infrastructure, the primary funding plan did not include funding for the recreational and community spaces that were central to the original planning documents.[66]

The revitalization will also introduce 399 affordable rental units (unsubsidized). The original plans proposed to construct 5,417 market-rate units and increase the overall population to approximately 12,500 residents. However, in 2013, TCHC requested approval from the Toronto City Council to increase the number of market units because the updated calculations revealed that the original plan fell short in its ability to generate enough money to sustain the project.[67] Despite pushback from residents, the city council approved the request to increase the construction of market units, which would shift the percentage of social housing units to 25 percent and market units to 75 percent as opposed to the previous balance of 40 percent and 60 percent, respectively.[68] While there are conflicting accounts about aspects of the financial model due to the partnership with private developers (and therefore limited public data on private profits), it is estimated that for every public dollar spent on the project, TCHC only yields $0.26 cents in profits from condo sales. (footnote: August, Speculating Social Housing, 130). The revitalization was meant to be self-financing, with sales of new market units covering the cost of replacing TCHC's subsidized apartments. But delays and flaws in the business model have led to shortfalls that the city must cover."[69] According to a 2019 city report, the estimated shortfall for Phases 4 and 5 of the revitalization is $182.1 million.[70]

By 2016, ten years into the revitalization process, 25 percent of residents' annual household income was below $19,999, 31 percent was between $20,000 and $49,999, 21 percent was between $50,000 and $79,999, 13 percent made between $80,000 and $124,999, and 10 percent made $125,000 or more.[71] The median household income increased by more than $20,000 since 2006 ($24,775) to $42,369. These income demographics will continue to shift with the completion of the final stages of revitalization.

Revitalizing Lawrence Heights

The *Lawrence-Allen Revitalization Plan* shares many characteristics of the Regent Park revitalization. The plan's genesis came in October 2005, when the city introduced the Neighborhood Action Plan (NAP), which designated Lawrence Heights as targeted for increased investment in infrastructure and community service improvements. Formerly known as "priority neighborhoods," these areas were determined based on a set of social risk factors identified in the 2001 Census. (Regent Park is not a priority neighborhood, primarily because it has more community service programs per capita than any other neighborhood in the city.)[72] The plan to revitalize Lawrence Heights was endorsed by the Toronto City Council in 2010; the developers were named in 2013 and the first phase of redevelopment began in 2015.

According to revitalization documents, the majority of residents in Lawrence Heights prior to revitalization were of West Indian and African descent, with a large population of English, Somali, Oromo, Amharic, and Spanish speakers. Lawrence Heights is known as a hub for Caribbean and East African communities in Toronto.[73] Prior to revitalization, the median income was approximately $15,000.[74] The revitalization plan calls for rebuilding all 1,208 units and adding approximately 5,500–6,300 market-rate units. The overall population of Lawrence Heights will increase to 16,000 upon completion of the buildings. Demolition for Phase 1 of the plan began in 2015 with estimated completion in 2023. The anticipated completion date for the revitalization is 2035.

According to TCHC, Lawrence Heights was selected for revitalization due to poor design, building decay, rising crime rates, and the concentration of low-income housing. The popular representations of Lawrence Heights in the media since the 1990s helped justify these descriptions. Lawrence Heights is popularly known throughout Toronto as "The Jungle."[75] "The Jungle" is described as isolated and maze-like.[76] It has a reputation, broadcast and promulgated in the local news media, as a center of crime, violence, poverty, racial tensions, and gang activity.[77] In 1994 a group of young men who lived in Lawrence Heights were involved in a robbery in Toronto's upscale Yorkville neighborhood, and one of them shot and killed a bystander, 23-year-old

Vivi Leimonis. The murder brought increased attention to Lawrence Heights and heightened already existing stigmatization. The extensive media coverage of the incident echoed previous sentiments about an isolated neighborhood filled with crime and violence.[78]

The revitalization of Lawrence Heights promised to address these issues. A May 2007 City of Toronto Staff Report from the deputy city manager addressed to the Affordable Housing Committee introduced an initiative to research opportunities to revitalize Lawrence Heights in conjunction with TCHC's findings.[79] The report promised "a comprehensive and integrated approach to the Lawrence Heights neighborhood revitalization that will incorporate social, physical, economic, environmental, health-related and community-based supports into a planning framework that will ultimately strengthen the community."[80] The report outlined a plan to tear down the housing project and replace it with mixed-income, mixed-tenure, and mixed-use housing and buildings. According to official city documents, the preferred plan "describes a mixed-income neighborhood which is park-centered, transit supportive, and well integrated with the broader city. Through public and private reinvestment, it provides for the replacement of all 1,208 existing social housing units along with 5,500 to 6,300 new market units."[81] The executive summary of the *Lawrence-Allen Revitalization Plan* introduced the coordinated efforts of the City of Toronto, TCHC, and the Toronto District School Board in producing a revitalization plan for the area.[82] It depicts the revitalization of Lawrence Heights as the "catalyst" to address the poverty and segregation of the neighborhood.

The *Lawrence-Allen Revitalization Plan* is organized around four key themes. "Reinvestment" in the Lawrence-Allen study area will "renew the social housing stock, develop new private housing, construct new public infrastructure, and cultivate a sustainable neighborhood."[83] The second theme, "Mobility," focuses on the need for a more integrated transportation system to better connect the area with surrounding neighborhoods and the rest of the city. Theme three, "Livability," promotes social integration and the fostering of social networks to ensure a high quality of life for residents. Finally, the last theme, "Place-Making," links the physical infrastructure to "civic and social life" to strengthen "community identity, promote public safety and foster vibrant public activity."[84]

The Lawrence Heights revitalization planning documents promise to make the area more integrated.[85] The Regent Park plan also references this aim, but it has greater urgency in Lawrence Heights, which lacks the same access to the infrastructure of the inner city. As such, the transportation network is a major theme of the Lawrence Heights revitalization. Another distinction is that Allen Road bisects Lawrence Heights—Regent Park has no corresponding challenge. Through the four themes, reinvestment, mobility, livability, and place-making, the plan brings Canadian ideals that promote and bring a healthy civic identity to the forefront.

Conclusion

In an era of neoliberal urbanism, the privatization of public space, public-private partnerships, decreases in funds to services to address urban inequality, and the link between private property and individual success are normalized in the transformation of cities and the revitalization of low-income neighborhoods. Under Toronto Mayor Rob Ford's notorious reign from 2010 to 2014, the city sold twenty-two public housing units in an effort to address financial strain and a maintenance and quality crisis. In 2015, it was reported that addressing the repair backlog and housing conditions of TCHC buildings and properties would cost the city $7.5 billion over thirty years.[86] Approximately 500 units have been boarded up because they were deemed uninhabitable. It is estimated that by 2023, an additional 7,500 units will be added to that number. Yet, between 2010 and 2020 the waitlist for social housing increased by 50 percent.[87] The waitlist between 2016 and 2021 remained at approximately 81,000 to 82,000 households.[88] The average wait time was an average of 8.4 years for a unit.[89] In 2021, TCHC announced the transfer of an additional 761 units to two land trusts as a key aspect in the implementation of the City of Toronto's Tenants First Plan.[90] Under the Tenants First Plan, the city aims to address TCHC's budgetary problems and maintenance backlog by shifting to a "more targeted housing portfolio." The plan identified what they labeled "scattered properties" across the city including single-family or multi-unit homes owned and managed by TCHC. Framed as a "transfer of public assets," the City of Toronto and TCHC continue to offload units and downsize their portfolio despite long housing waitlists.[91] This housing shortage is the result of neoliberal policies and reflects the disparity that is (re)produced by the alignment of policy with capital accumulation and the commodification of housing.

Toronto has failed to address the interconnections between a housing shortage, affordable and adequate housing, and economic and income inequality. The Toronto Foundation's annual *Vital Signs Report* tracks the health and well-being of Torontonians and inequality across the city. Its 2021 report documents that in the past ten to fifteen years, home prices have increased by 213 percent, and there is an increase in food insecurity with approximately 30 percent of Indigenous and Black households experiencing food insecurity.[92] The 2019 pre-pandemic *Vital Signs Report* reports a 69 percent increase in sheltered houseless peoples over five years.[93] A report by Toronto Public Health highlights that "the gap between rich and poor people in Toronto has been growing steadily since 1980. Between 1980 and 2005, income inequality in Toronto increased by 31 [percent], more than any other major Canadian city. In 2012, 15 percent of all income in Toronto went to the 1 percent of people who earned the most."[94] Income inequality is defined by the uneven distribution of income across a population. The 2016 census documents that 20.2 percent of Toronto families were low income. In Toronto, income inequality is intertwined with residential segregation and racial inequality: "In high-income neighborhoods, 73 percent of residents are White compared to only 31 percent in low-income neighborhoods, and this has become more concentrated over time."[95] The segregation is attributed to an increase in "inflation-adjusted average income" for white people in Toronto.[96] Incomes have grown by 60 percent for the white population compared to just 1 percent for those racialized as nonwhite. Relatedly, income segregation by neighborhood increased by 56 percent between 1990 and 2015.[97] In 2015, nonwhite Torontonians made fifty-two cents for every dollar earned by their white neighbors.[98]

Between 2010 and 2020, housing costs in Toronto grew four times faster than income, with rent, specifically, growing two times faster than income.[99] A 2019 analysis of the Toronto housing market revealed that "Toronto needs to access about 150,000 bedrooms to free up renters stuck in overcrowded conditions. Toronto needs new social housing units to relieve the 122,250 households in the private rental market with incomes <$30,000 living in units renting at $750 or more" and "31.6% of renter family households live in unsuitable housing."[100] According to the Royal Bank of Canada, in 2022, Toronto homebuyers would need pretax income of $240,000 to afford a mortgage at the benchmark price ($1,250,000).[101]

The neoliberal urban revitalization of Toronto's Regent Park and Lawrence Heights is positioned to counter the ongoing challenges of urban poverty and housing affordability and as the obvious way to address an outdated approach to social housing. However, high rates of housing vulnerability and limited access to affordable housing mark the limited nature of neoliberal approaches that put profit and privatization before people. The revitalization of Regent Park and Lawrence Heights reflects the variety of ways neoliberal logic operates alongside multicultural policy, and practices and obscures the structural causes of racial and class inequality with a neoliberal market-driven solution. Reflecting on revitalization in Toronto, Horak and Moore argue, "A confluence of factors has recently driven neighborhood revitalization onto the policy agenda, yet this has occurred in a broader setting where opportunities for the political expression of neighborhood-level social concerns are very weak and where relevant institutional and fiscal capacity is fragmented."[102] While revitalization has been constructed as the go-to planning approach to address the many shortcomings of social and public housing, as I will show in the following chapters, revitalization frameworks are both limited and deceiving in their potential to create transformation and address inequality.

Precarious Mosaic

Diversity or Disparity in Toronto's Regent Park?

> The main theme that links all of the elements of this plan together
> is the importance of striving for diversity as a key organizing feature
> of the revitalization process: diversity of building types, designs and
> heights; diversity of tenures; diversity and mix of incomes; diversity
> and mix of uses; diversity of builders; and diversity of activities. A
> successful Toronto neighbourhood reflects this type of diversity. It
> is also what will make Regent Park a successful and special place.
>
> —REGENT PARK COLLABORATIVE TEAM, *Regent Park Revitalization
> Study*, 5

This passage from the *Regent Park Revitalization Study* seems almost comical
in its employment of diversity talk. Official narratives of Toronto's overarching identity claim that its multicultural and diverse population is the city's
defining feature.[1] The Toronto coat of arms displays the city's motto: "Diversity Our Strength." While the motto originally referred to the diversity
among the six municipalities that were amalgamated in the late 1990s,
contemporary observers, as well as those who invoke the motto, often use it
to refer to Toronto's "cultural diversity."

Chapter 2 examines the uses of the term "diversity" in the revitalization
framework of Regent Park. Official descriptions of Canada's multicultural
population often use the term diversity as a signal of pride. Given the understanding that Toronto represents the pinnacle of Canadian multiculturalism, it is no surprise that the concept of diversity stands out as a central
feature of the revitalization planning framework in Regent Park. What is cu-
rious, however, is the use of diversity to refer to multiple planning priorities in the revitalization project beyond cultural diversity.

The primary concern of the revitalization planning framework in Regent
Park is to address the segregation of the housing project and integrate the
Regent Park community into the broader social fabric of Toronto. To achieve
integration, the revitalization planning documents emphasize a symbiosis
between three types of diversity: diversity of use, diversity of income and tenure, and diversity of culture. For example, in the *Regent Park Social Development*

Plan, planners suggest, "After decades of planning and organizing on the part of tenants and stakeholders, Regent Park is being rebuilt as a diverse, mixed-income community in an open and integrated neighbourhood."[2] I explore how the interchangeable and often confusing references to diversity attempt to align a diversity of income, use, and culture with Canadian multicultural ideals in order to legitimize the neoliberal revitalization project, yet do little to address income inequality or segregation. I argue that the diversity of diversities is precariously constructed as a tool that legitimates the revitalization project.

In the revitalization of Regent Park, the multiple and often ambiguous uses of diversity align diversity to a presupposed success and the promotion of social inclusion in Canada's liberal democratic and multicultural society. I suggest that the use of diversity becomes a legitimating tactic because diversity hinges upon the cachet of multiculturalism in Canadian society by tapping into the ideology and discourses of multiculturalism. While both diversity and "mix" are generally taken for granted in planning discourse (diversity of income or use and mixed-income or use), such terms should be analyzed more closely and in relation to the contexts in which they are employed. In Toronto, using the term diversity (as opposed to mixed) to characterize the key features of the planning framework allows the revitalization to align with and draw on the cachet of Canadian multiculturalism. This alignment operates by normalizing a mirage of diversity (diversity of income, diversity of use, and diversity of culture) that characterizes the integrative features of the revitalization. Regent Park revitalization documents employ the standard planning terms of "mixed use" and "mixed income" interchangeably with "diversity of use" and "diversity of income." The strange shift from mix to diversity is not neutral. I show that the use of diversity to refer to use and income is a signaling process—it positions the revitalization project such that it is productively aligned with a broader set of Canadian values about inclusion and an acceptance of cultural diversity. These uses of diversity and mix align because of expectations that we should accept cultural and racial differences in Canadian society.

Building on the work of scholars critical of the uses of the concept of diversity in employment policy, education, communities, and law, I suggest that because of the ambiguous and precarious usage of the term, diversity can signal equity and the inclusion of diverse ethnoracial groups and low-income residents under the auspices of goodwill and multiculturalism; but it does not challenge the historical and structural causes of racial and class disparity.[3] There is nothing stable about how diversity and multiculturalism operate—hence a precarious mosaic.

It is not particularly novel to assert that diversity is a contested concept; indeed, diversity is a constantly shifting construction and difficult to tie to a particular meaning.[4] While diversity is increasingly used to refer to multiple signifiers of identity (e.g., age, gender, sexuality, ability), this chapter will use its more traditional meaning—related to race, ethnicity, and socioeconomic class.[5] However, I challenge the popular construction of diversity as emerging from bodies and subjectivity and instead understand diversity as constructed from modes of governance. In *On Being Included: Racism and Diversity in Institutional Life*, Sara Ahmed investigates the institutionalization of diversity in higher education and explores "what diversity does by focusing on what diversity obscures, that is by focusing on the relationship between diversity and racism as a way of making explicit a tendency that is reproduced by staying implicit."[6] I draw from Ahmed's insights to shed light on what is obscured and reproduced in the implementation of diversity in revitalization. The following section examines the uses of the three types of diversity to highlight how a diversity of diversities operates in the planning logic as a key legitimizing tool for the revitalization of Regent Park.[7]

The Diversity of Diversities

Diversity of Use

The Pam McConnell Aquatic Center (formerly the Regent Park Aquatic Center), named after late local City Councilor Pam McConnell, received media attention because of its swim hours for women and trans people. In the *New York Times* article referenced in the introduction, the journalist boasts, "On Saturday evenings, mechanized screens shroud the center's expansive glass walls to create a session that allows only women and girls to relax in the hot tub, swim laps or careen down the water slide, a rare bit of 'me' time treasured by many of the neighborhood's Muslim residents."[8] And, "The aquatic center reflects that ethos of inclusion. After the weekly women's swim ends, the blinds stay down for a private session popular with transgender people who want to swim without feeling they are being stared at. Out of the pool, everyone uses gender-neutral locker rooms that provide private cubicles for changing."[9] The aquatic center, a facility that provides services at no cost to the public, is just one example of how recreational and other uses were introduced into the neighborhood. While the revitalization plans posit a diversity of incomes as central to the financial framework of the revitalization, they posit a diversity of use as the means to bring and support businesses, services, recreational spaces, and employment opportunities that serve people across different cultural groups. The employment of the term diversity of use—or mixed use—in this context aligns more closely with a diversity of amenities as opposed to more conventional land use. For example, the *Regent Park Revitalization Study* suggests that revitalization will "provide opportunities for the community to celebrate and share its diverse cultures. It would provide spaces for economic regeneration, educational programs, community gardens, recreational activities and arts and cultural programs."[10] This section examines how the term diversity is employed to describe a mix of uses and what, exactly, makes a diversity of use *diverse*.

A neighborhood with a diversity of use incorporates residential dwellings, commercial spaces, parks, and community spaces as opposed to the concentration of only residential dwellings (a central critique to the design of public housing in the twentieth century). The planning documents lament that Regent Park lacked commercial establishments for residents to shop, eat, interact, and find local employment opportunities prior to revitalization.[11] For example, the *Regent Park Revitalization Study* notes that "Regent Park is an almost completely residential neighbourhood, targeted to lower income households, unlike a typical downtown neighbourhood, which has a wide range of uses, building types and mix of tenures."[12] I explore how the employment of a diversity of use insists on particular uses managed under the revitalization (particularly large commercial retailers) and reinforces a critique that a diversity of uses makes the neighborhood desirable for those who own market units.

In Regent Park, the revitalization introduced the new aquatic center, athletic fields, Daniels Spectrum (an arts and culture hub), a new community center, and commercial and retail storefronts. Four years into the Regent Park revitalization, new businesses began to open on Parliament Street, which borders the neighborhood to the west. By 2010, Rogers Communications (mobile phone and internet provider), the Royal Bank of Canada, Sobeys Fresh Co. (the more affordable Sobey's grocery store), and Tim Horton's coffee shop were all serving residents. These commercial spaces are on the first level of One Cole Condominiums (a market-rate building), which were built in Phase 1 of the revitalization.[13] While the contracts for the real estate included a commitment to local hiring (and reports document that

"378 jobs were created through revitalization partnerships with businesses/ agencies"), some residents were concerned that these large corporations would not improve the neighborhood and were a sign of gentrification.[14] There were also concerns around jobs being long-term and full-time given many of them would be in construction and trades during the redevelopment process.[15] Chandra, a former resident who worked at the local health center and lived on the border of Regent Park at the time of our interview, discussed how gentrification was becoming increasingly visible: "You are starting to see it around, you know. Restaurants that used to serve the folks that are here are gone or closed [or] have been moved and replaced by places that have menus that are inaccessible to low-income people or won't let them sit there. You know. So, you are seeing it around you. You know, I saw it in my backyard before, when they took down the button factory that was behind me and they put a Mercedes showroom in."[16] Chandra was not specific about which venues were not accessible or did not permit residents to "sit there," and there is a lack of data on the number of businesses that closed or were displaced in the revitalization. In the case of the newly opened Tim Horton's, for example, it is well known that Tim Horton's is affordable, but it is unclear if residents were discouraged from sitting in the coffee shop. Chandra's reference to the Mercedes showroom that opened in close proximity to Regent Park (across the Don Valley Parkway) was seen to be representative of the threat of gentrification that was closing in on Regent Park. Moreover, Chandra's reflections on a diversity of use should not be understood apart from the history of Regent Park as a stigmatized and racially segregated neighborhood or apart from the gentrification of the neighborhoods to the north, east, and south of Regent Park. In the context of revitalization, diversifying the use of a neighborhood might push out a restaurant or business that formerly anchored a community. In theory, a diversity of use should not necessarily facilitate the closing of local businesses, and in the case of Regent Park, a diversity of use was positioned as a tool to integrate the neighborhood into the surrounding social fabric. However, given the role of the commercial partnerships among the Daniels Corporation, TCHC, and Sobey's, Rogers, and Royal Bank of Canada, a diversity of use seems to insist on particular uses or particular partnerships with large corporations.[17]

One community agency executive director, Andrea, who was recruited by TCHC to help support the consultation efforts in Regent Park, described tensions around the planning process and a diversity of use: "It is this idea that this stuff that is being brought in, you know, there's an arts and cultural center; there's a learning center; there is going to be an aquatics center with a covered pool; there's a big park which has a number of things. There are a lot of new public facilities. There is a new community center. These are all being brought in because there is going to be mixed income. But why didn't you do that for us before? We have been here a lot longer." Andrea's critique questions the place of diversity of use in the revitalization efforts and why resources and amenities were not provided to public housing residents before revitalization. She went on to say, "You are only doing this for them (the market units). You are not doing it for us. So that is an underlying current, a theme, that is always there and it is difficult."[18] While she acknowledges the need for services and amenities, her comments shed light on the long-standing precarity of Regent Park residents and the notion that investment is being made in the neighborhood to serve and make the neighborhood desirable for middle-income residents. A 2019 article in the *Toronto Star*, "Regent Park Residents Say They Can't Access Their Neighbourhood Pool: City Data Backs Them Up," aligns with Andrea's concerns that the introduction of new facilities would not necessarily serve residents and Chandra's argument about the accessibility of the new mixed-use additions to the neighborhood.[19] According to the article, "only about a quarter of the registrations at the aquatic center for the most recent fall/winter session of city-run programs were for registrants whose home address was in Regent Park or the area immediately surrounding it."[20]

Andrea also described a situation about the planning of a new learning center in Regent Park: "So, for instance, the whole thing around the learning center that is in the first building on Dundas, that came out to us by a presentation that one of the senior TCHC people did, who is responsible for buildings, and he just talked about well there's going to be a University of Toronto learning center here. And there were six of us around the table who provide literacy and adult ed courses and nobody had been consulted or anything. We didn't know anything about it."[21] Andrea is referring to the Regent Park Centre of Learning that opened in 2010. The learning center provides college preparation courses, learning circles for women, computer literacy, and civic engagement opportunities for residents. Andrea's frustration was a result of not being consulted on the new center, particularly because many service providers in the area provide the same type of programming with limited resources. This includes the similarly named Regent Park Learning Centre, where I worked as a tutor, that was formerly housed in one of the low-rise buildings at 217 Gerrard Street and run by one of the community's most well-known service providers, Dixon Hall. The development of the Regent Park Centre of Learning is one example of how the mixed-use framework ignored existing programming, missed opportunities to develop key local partnerships, and is tied to Chandra's claims that the revitalization forced small businesses to close because of an insistence on particular types of uses that were specifically sponsored or initiated by the revitalization.

While certainly the Aquatic Centre and Daniels Spectrum are important additions to the community and provide space for culturally diverse residents in Regent Park (diversity of use/ mix of use that takes cultural diversity into account), they obscure both the role of corporate retail and commercial space (as opposed to local small businesses or storefronts and the previously existing Regent Park Learning Centre) and the neoliberal revitalization framework. As Kipfer and Petrunia suggest, the revitalization of Regent Park "is not only a product of state rescaling (in this case, the downloading of public housing to the local state) and a new phase of state-managed gentrification. The project is promoted primarily by exponents of downtown progressivism and circumscribed by the ambiguous political horizon of the metropolitan mainstream. In this context, we suggest that the redevelopment project of Regent Park is a multipronged, racialized strategy to recolonize a segregated and long-pathologized, but potentially valuable central city space in the name of diversity and social mixity."[22] A diversity of use in relation to diversity of income and culture can become part of a mask for gentrification, whereby the entire fabric of the neighborhood is altered to favor private investment and the dismantling of public provisions. This guise of inclusion further entrenches racism and classism. Andrea's reflection that "you are only doing this for them (the market units); you are not doing it for us" is a critique of the mixed-use facilities that attract new middle-income residents and private investment.[23] While women-and-trans-only swim hours are an important step and much needed in Regent Park, the overall diversity of use framework does not indicate that the uses are in fact significantly diverse at all or implemented in a way that builds on and contributes to existing community infrastructure.

Diversity of Income

Scholars have explored the social implications of mixed-income communities as well as how the term "mixed income" is defined in different ways.[24] For example, Mark L. Joseph, Robert J. Chaskin, and Henry S. Webber argue that proposals for mixed-income housing are a policy response to urban poverty.[25] They find that the logic of mixed-income housing is based on four propositions: the establishment of social networks that encompass the social capital of middle-class people; the presence of higher-income residents to raise the level of social control; the dispersal of middle-class values to lower-class neighbors; and the superior ability to attract business development and other resources. Many scholars argue, however, that mixed-income developments rarely live up to their promise of inclusion.[26] Chaskin and Joseph assert that one of the expectations of mixed-income housing is the expansion of social networks and opportunities for low-income communities.[27] Yet, they argue that this expectation does not necessarily match residents' experiences or lead to the desired outcome.[28]

Contemporary revitalization schemes in Toronto that employ a mixed-income approach must be further contextualized in relation to changes in social housing policy in Canada in the 1990s as outlined in the previous chapter.[29] Because of these neoliberal changes to housing policy, new local public housing providers were forced to seek solutions to address affordable housing shortages and maintenance repair backlogs in Toronto. As such, revitalization was one of the first major initiatives brought forth by the Toronto Community Housing Corporation (TCHC). In a report by Derek Ballantyne, the CEO of TCHC, to the Board of Directors, he noted, "The proposed housing mix was driven by the aim to effectively end the isolation of Regent Park residents from the surrounding communities, and to meet the principles of a mixed community developed with residents through the planning process."[30] Such mixed-income frameworks are certainly not unique to Toronto. TCHC examined models from the United States, Europe, and the St. Lawrence redevelopment in Toronto to inform the mixed-income model for Regent Park.[31] In Regent Park, TCHC entered a joint venture with The Daniels Corporation, a large real estate developer in Toronto (in 2020, a new developer, Tridel, was selected to step in to complete the final two phases of the revitalization). The funding for the $1 billion-plus project in Regent Park was provided by sales of market housing, TCHC savings from maintenance, and city funding for public infrastructure, as well as provincial and federal funding.[32] While the selling of market-rate units by private developers funded the new TCHC housing stock, funding from the City of Toronto, Province of Ontario, and federal government was primarily responsible for the public infrastructure improvements (e.g., roads, sewers, parks, etc.).[33] Leroy, a TCHC representative in Regent Park, described the mixed-income approach as the solution to making the neighborhood "a far more functional part of the city."[34]

A diversity of incomes (mixed-income) and tenures provides both the financial backing for the projects but also aims to address the social isolation of segregated housing projects.[35] In this section, I suggest diversity of income and tenure is framed to address urban inequality and social isolation of the communities, but because of the diverse uses of diversity, it does not have to address the structural causes of such inequality and segregation. Instead, in the case of income, disparity of incomes is positioned as a diversity of incomes, and a diversity of incomes is positioned as something to value, not as something to eliminate. Additionally, a diversity of incomes obscures the removal of a percentage of public housing units to other neighborhoods and the overall decrease in public housing units in Regent Park because of a perception of "too much social housing."[36] So, for example, 266 rent-geared-to-income (RGI) units were moved off the footprint of Regent Park, leaving 1,817 on site. And 5,417 units will be market units, making the percentage of market units approximately one-quarter of the total units, with a total of 7,234 units overall.[37] The maximum percentage of social housing to compose an adequate social mix was set at changed to 25 percent (with 75 percent market units).[38]

TCHC's *Regent Park Social Development Plan* emphasizes the importance of diversity of income and tenure:

> In July 2003, Toronto City Council approved the plan for revitalization of Regent Park. This approval opened the way to a period of significant transition and change. Council gave direction . . . [for] a Social Development Plan for Regent Park to help address issues of transition and social inclusion. The redevelopment of Regent Park will replace existing housing but will also bring in new market housing. This will add to the existing population of Regent Park. It will also add to the *diversity of the population* [emphasis added], introducing a *broader mix of income and tenure* [emphasis added]. This can provide significant advantages to the people now living in Regent Park. The resources of their community grow with the growing *diversity* [emphasis added] of their neighbourhood, creating the potential for new relationships and new opportunities.[39]

Here, diversity is not specifically attached to income, use, or culture, but in general as a "diversity of population" and "the growing diversity of their neighbourhood." However, in both uses of diversity, it is meant to signal the diversity of income that the plans introduce. A diversity of diversities converges through a promotion of the various types of diversity and the opportunities the revitalization makes available. The first use of the term diversity in the section from the social development plan referenced above is in relation to a mix of income and tenure and is framed as adding to the diversity of the population by aligning it with "a broader mix of income and tenure." While the social development plan describes Regent Park as culturally diverse by referencing the linguistic and cultural diversity of the neighborhood, it describes it as lacking diversity of income.[40] For example, in section 3.2, the plan presents a "snapshot" of the current neighborhood and provides the statistics on new immigrants and linguistic diversity. It references Regent Park as the "lowest-income census tract in Ontario."[41] It also suggests, "When the redevelopment proposal is realized, people with a variety of incomes and housing needs will be living in Regent Park," in contrast to the current lack of income diversity.[42]

In these examples from the social development plan, diversity is used to signal income.[43] The claim that diversity will bring "new opportunities" refers to the general logic that legitimizes mixed-income frameworks and suggests that the social capital of the middle class will provide opportunities as well as businesses that are attracted by their purchasing power.[44] This framing of diversity hinges on diversity's cachet in Canada—linking diversity to income and the introduction of market-rate housing, with no indication of what new relationships and new opportunities it will present to the already culturally diverse neighborhood. This is one example of how a disparity of incomes is framed as a diversity of incomes in the revitalization.

When asked about the mixed-income framework, Amanda, an urban planner in Toronto, suggested, "Well I think that's [pause] part of the problem. And you know it applies anywhere really: *too much of one thing is not good* [emphasis added] . . . so it is providing that variety in a community. I think that is important. You used to come into Regent Park and you know that you were someplace different. It didn't integrate with the rest of the fabric [of the city] . . . *I just think that you can't have too much of a good thing or then having too much is a bad thing* [emphasis added] . . . and then, it is looking for creating a mixture that I think that will help."[45] "Too much" of "one thing" refers to a concentration of people at one income level. However, her reflection implies that the concentration is only bad if it is a concentration of low-income people. Planners were not proposing to diversify or add income mixture to middle-income neighborhoods. Amanda suggested that introducing a diversity of income would make it possible to integrate the neighborhood into the fabric of the city.[46] But her rhetoric gets messy when she says, "I just think that you can't have too much of a good thing or then having too much is a bad thing." Her reflection that "you used to come into Regent Park and you know that you were someplace different," in relation to "too much of one thing is not good," suggests the ways that Regent Park was stigmatized for both its racial and low-income segregation from the rest of the city. The racial and class segregation was central to the formation and stigmatization of mid-twentieth-century public housing projects.[47] The outdated planning model, that promoted inward facing buildings and no through-streets was a mechanism of spatial and racial separation that has long-standing material effects on public housing residents. Under urban revitalization, a diversity of income is one tool to address this segregation. Amanda signals diversity when she argues that "creating a mixture" will address "too much" concentration.

Race and racial segregation are obscured in Amanda's response; her references to "knowing you were somewhere different" and the lack of integration with the rest of Toronto, however, must consider the history of racial segregation in public housing in order to understand the specific dynamics at play. Because of a concentration of low-income people of color, racial and cultural diversity are a problem to be solved, in contrast to the Canadian ideals promoted by multiculturalism that suggest diversity is something to celebrate and honor. The language of "knowing you were someplace different" and "didn't integrate with the rest of the city" position the racial and cultural diversity of Regent Park that existed before revitalization as a problem to be solved in contrast to the revitalization's insistence on diversity. The vague reference to creating a "mixture" allows for the history of racism and classism to be obscured by the general promotion of diversity in Canada's liberal democracy.

The financial plan that supported the revitalization depended on the public-private partnership and the selling of market-value units to generate revenue to fund the revitalization—a testimony to the result of 1990s neoliberal restructuring.[48] The rhetoric of the plans described the mixed-income framework as not only funding the project, but also adding to the diversity of the population by bringing in middle-class homebuyers and those from higher economic status to formerly low-income neighborhoods in order to influence the behavior of low-income residents.[49] In the *Regent Park Revitalization Study*, the authors list the perceived benefits of mixed-income housing: "Mixed-income housing is seen as an antidote to the conditions of social and economic isolation brought about by traditional public housing development. Behavioural patterns of lower-income tenants will be altered by interaction with higher-income neighbors. For example, social norms about workforce participation will be passed on to the low-income residents. The crime rate will fall as high-income residents enforce stricter ground rule for the community."[50] Therefore, a diversity of incomes not only provides financial backing for the rejuvenation of the deteriorated public housing stock, but also a perceived opportunity to change the social demographics of the community by bringing in middle-income families. One of the perceived benefits to this demographic shift is influencing the behavior of low-income residents.[51] Urban anthropologist Ryan James critiques the mixed-income model: "The unstated assumption is that these are the model citizens of the neoliberal city, and that their uprightness will hopefully rub off on public housing residents once they live side-by-side."[52] Instead of focusing on the structural causes of poverty and eliminating income disparity, this paternalistic framing and underlying classist insistence that people with low-income need to change their behaviors, undermines the long-standing social networks and sustainable community practices (e.g., child care, community events, local markets) in public housing and focuses on the perceived moral failures of those who live in public housing. Further, according to Daniel J. Rowe and James R. Dunn's 2011–2012 research on tenure and income mix in Regent Park,

> There was evidence only of modest interaction between tenures, and even relatively little interaction among residents of the same tenure (i.e., among condominium residents or among social housing residents). For most of the residents, the "mixed" nature of the community was a positive, if peripheral, aspect of the redevelopment, with condominium residents espousing more vocal support for the strategy of tenure mix than subsidized renters. For most of the subsidized tenants, more proximal concerns about building management and aspects of the physical condition of their units took precedence over tenure mix, although none directly expressed antipathy towards this strategy or towards the condominium owners in the community.[53]

While a diversity of incomes proposed to increase interactions between residents of different incomes and tenures to influence behavior and create opportunities, there is little evidence to support that such interactions occur in the first place. Notably, Rowe and Dunn reported that owners and middle-income residents were "more vocal" about supporting a diversity of incomes than renters, and that residents living in subsidized housing were more concerned with the "building management" and the condition of their units (they complained about the condition of their housing).[54] As Ashley Spalding highlights, neoliberal ideologies about the culture of poverty legitimize deconcentration and ignore structural causes of poverty and instead focus on individual merit as the cause of and solution to poverty.[55] As such, mixed-income frameworks are promoted as a solution to address urban poverty by both diluting the population of low-income residents and asserting that the social capital of middle-income people will help "elevate" low-income people and increase their social networks, opportunities for employment, and the spread of middle-class values. However, as planning scholar Martine August asserts, Regent Park residents reported that they missed their old, more spacious homes and that the new mixed-income development had a negative impact on their social networks and community bonds.[56] Further, there is evidence that a diversity of incomes has a negative impact on social and political networks in Regent Park, whereby public housing residents become politically marginalized as a result of the revitalization despite decades of intricate and powerful tenant activism.[57] As August and Alan Walks argue, "The evidence points to a future of political marginalisation and exclusion rather than the social harmony promised by normative discourses of social mix."[58] Additionally, the use of diversity legitimizes an argument that income mixing in and of itself is "good." To reiterate, disparity of incomes is positioned as a diversity of incomes and thus a diversity of incomes is positioned as something to value, not as something to challenge or eliminate. A diversity of incomes frames income inequality as an achievement to be celebrated without calling into question the structures that produce income inequality or structural solutions to racial and class inequality and residential segregation.

Diversity of Culture

In the planning process, a diversity of income and use is closely tied to a diversity of culture. The *Regent Park Social Development Plan* notes that "the cultural diversity of Regent Park requires a range of considerations to ensure that the space available to the community reflects the needs of the cultural and faith groups."[59] It also notes that "ethno-specific shopping opportunities can also serve this function if the facilities offer a 'boutique' setting that appeals to a wide variety of potential shoppers, who may be initially unfamiliar with the products but attracted to new cultural opportunities."[60] A diversity of culture in the planning process most explicitly signals a commitment to Canadian multiculturalism. Canadian multicultural discourses frame different cultures and cultural practices as something to be celebrated or honored and shared with society. A celebration of cultures, or "celebrating diversity," is a common Canadian idiom that conveys the positive associations with different cultural groups and the state's commitment to recognizing different cultural traditions and practices (in opposition to an assimilationist model).

Reference to a diversity of culture in the planning documents and by planners in interviews was inconsistent. In some cases, planners and the planning documents described culture as something to be preserved and celebrated in Regent Park. In other cases, a celebration of culture was described as something that would be ushered in via revitalization and a diversity of income and use. These inconsistencies index how diversity is ambiguously employed and, in fact, undermines any efforts to address structural inequality and racism and disparity along the lines of race and class. Further, a promotion of cultural diversity in the revitalization process commodifies "culture" in relation to a diversity of income and use. A diversity of culture becomes something to be consumed, particularly because of new middle-income owners and via promotions of markets or bazaars (markets have existed in Regent Park for decades and are certainly not new because of revitalization). For example, the *Regent Park Revitalization Study* suggests that "the vibrant cultural mix and the young entrepreneurial demographic of Regent Park offer an opportunity to create a unique market or 'bazaar.'"[61] The phrasing "offer an opportunity to create" positions culture as something to commodify under revitalization but also ignores the organic and sustainable local economies that preexist the revitalization. As City of Toronto employee Corinne reported:

> You know the research will say that mixed-income communities are a good approach, because the concentration of low-income people is no longer seen as the best way to plan it. But you have to do it with the appropriate facilities and services and that sort of thing . . . and we are in a diverse city, so you obviously want to do that. But it is building on the wealth of opportunity. I think we will see lots of things culturally, cultural celebrations, the sharing of cultural traditions. *You probably will see markets and things like that developing over time* [emphasis added]. So, I think that is sort of inherent within the plan. That is something that everyone desires to see. And the arts and cultural components are very clear, and we will have the arts and cultural center. There'll be a *cultural component* [emphasis added]. How do you honor the history of a very rich diverse cultural community as it changes and you're bringing in new people? So that is an element that we definitely want to kind of monitor and ensure is understood through consultation processes, and that actually comes through in the delivery of services.[62]

Corinne's reflection that "I think we will see lots of things culturally, cultural celebrations, the sharing of cultural traditions; you probably will see markets and things like that developing over time" is just one example of how a planner imagined the ways revitalization would promote cultural diversity. These insights suggest that a diversity of culture is something that can be promoted via revitalization and as something new, erasing a long history of markets and cultural celebrations in Regent Park. However, on the other hand, Corinne went on to ask, "How do you honor the history of a very rich diverse cultural community as it changes and you're bringing in new people?" Her question acknowledges the perceived challenges that come with a mixing of incomes in historically segregated neighborhoods. But her language of "honoring" the cultural diversity does not necessarily mean preserving cultural diversity. Further, in this case, the cultural diversity of the community is framed as something in the past ("how do you honor the history"), unlike her previous comments about seeing markets develop in the future. Corinne's reference to culture in relation to the new residents echoes the ways that cultural diversity can be commodified through revitalization efforts. Although Corinne does specifically reference a diverse cultural community, she does not refer to the racial diversity of Regent Park. Instead, culture can signal race without having to use the terms race or racism. As Cheryl Teelucksingh argues, "Celebrated Canadian markers of racial diversity and racial harmony that are spatially managed through systems of domination are in fact commodified versions of multiculturalism in the forms of 'ethnic culture,' ethnic neighborhoods, and 'ethnic restaurants.' Easily consumed and packaged versions of race in Canadian cities have been used to market and strengthen Canada's position in the global economy."[63] Here, Teelucksingh unpacks how racial diversity is tied to "systems of domination" and cannot be separated from racial inequality. In fact, these "easily consumed and packaged versions of race" are not only marketing tools that rely on the cachet of multiculturalism, but reify the construction of race and do not necessarily have to address racism and racial inequality. By focusing on culture and diversity, the plans avoid addressing the racial and class segregation that the revitalization aims to fix by "integrating" Regent Park into the surrounding urban fabric. Corinne's reflections not only erase the history of organic cultural celebrations in Regent Park, but also mark the commodification of multiculturalism that Teelucksingh flags as being tied to power, domination, and settler colonialism.

City planner Amanda described the relationship between the types of diversity: "So I think the mixing of the other elements [of use and income] will just sort of naturally play out so that we're going to see that cultural mixing." In this example, a diversity of incomes and diversity of uses will enable further cultural mixing but obscure the history of cultural diversity (and "mixing") in Regent Park. Unlike diversity of culture, which has a long history in Regent Park, the diversity of use and income were both central to the revitalization financial framework and introduced via the planning process. In this instance, I suggest that the diversity of diversities allows the implementation of use and income "diversity" to be framed as natural and are tools to legitimize the revitalization, hinging on diversity's social cachet in Canada. However, a careful reading of the multiple usages of diversity shows how diversity does not require the revitalization to address inequality and segregation in the way it suggests. Instead, by relying on diversity's social cachet in relation to multiculturalism, diversity can signal inclusion and integration but actually maintain disparity.

Conclusion

> Diversity, and particularly the notion of social mixing, now operate as code words to incorporate and submerge racialized public housing tenants under a cohesive form of normalcy defined by private property and the (middle-class and typically white) sensibilities of the "new normal": gentrified Victorian neighbourhoods and neomodernist condominium districts in central Toronto.
>
> —KIPFER AND PETRUNIA, "Recolonization and Public Housing," 121

What surfaces in this investigation are the ways a diversity of diversities operates as a legitimizing tactic to support the merits of the revitalization. So, for example, diversity of incomes is framed under a logic that it adds to the economic health of a community and is a solution to the concentration of poverty. A proposed benefit of a diversity of income is that it will expand the social networks of residents with low income and create economic opportunities; the mixing of incomes will allow for people with low incomes to climb the economic ladder.

However, as many scholars have shown, the evidence challenges the outcome that social networks expand or that mixed-income frameworks actually address inequality.[64] As I suggest, because of the value placed on the term diversity in relation to Canadian multiculturalism, diversity of incomes actually accepts income disparity as something to value as opposed to eliminate. It also obscures the dilution of social housing in the name of a diversity of incomes or social mixing. Importantly, there is an underlying assumption that a concentration of wealth is unproblematic as compared to a concentration of poverty. A mixed-income redevelopment framework targets and stigmatizes low-income neighborhoods — middle- and upper-income neighborhoods are not seen as in need of income mixing or diversification.

Like a diversity of income, diversity of use is also constructed as a strategy to address the segregation of the neighborhoods and integrate the neighborhoods into the surrounding social fabric. Diversity of use promotes retail, commercial, and recreational spaces alongside residential use. The proposed benefits include bringing more amenities to the neighborhood and contributing to the financial framework of the plan. Corinne, who worked on revitalization for the City of Toronto, alluded to the significance of mixed-use and mixed-income revitalization frameworks: "So those are the types of the communities [mixed-use and mixed-income] that we are trying to build and just essentially to knit into the fabric of the surrounding city and make it a healthy, successful, prosperous environment."[65] Corrine's omission of cultural diversity positions racial and ethnic diversity as separate from income and use. Further, as I have outlined, a diversity of use has promoted large corporate retailers, with little space for local/small businesses, and limited efforts to partner with existing businesses and service providers. Chandra argued that in fact, the diversity of use via revitalization was a sign of gentrification.

Lastly, references to a diversity of culture were inconsistent throughout the planning documents and interviews with planners. On the one hand, some planners argued that revitalization could create space for markets and cultural celebrations without reference to the already vibrant cultural life in Regent Park, while on the other hand they suggested that existing cultural diversity adds value to the revitalization.[66] In both cases, diversity is something to be managed by the plan, ignoring residents' experiences that have historically shaped the neighborhood. The management of a diversity of culture in the plans also does not acknowledge the ways that perceived and constructed racial differences in the housing projects are tied to structural inequality and stigmatization that have historically produced segregated communities. A diversity of culture easily aligns with a promotion of Canadian multiculturalism and legitimizes the revitalization efforts without specifically mentioning racism and histories of racial segregation. By relying on "diversity speak" and the cachet of Canadian multiculturalism, revitalization does not have to address the interlocking systems of domination that produced the segregation of the neighborhoods. In the case of Regent Park, "the Plan redeploys a conventional version of multiculturalism to manage the very racialized class disparities created by a project that is willing to sacrifice one type of diversity (the existing wealth of ethnolinguistic multiplicity) for the benefit of forms of diversity (measured in terms of income and housing tenure) that are compatible with gentrification."[67] The diversity of diversities as well as the interchangeability of mix and diversity are central to the revitalization projects and their perceived integrative features. Diversity is constructed and employed to signal the promise of inclusion by relying on the powerful cachet of multiculturalism in Canada. By shifting back and forth between use/income/culture and mix/diversity, a celebration of diversity is implied but, in fact, obscures and distracts from the structural problems the revitalization cannot solve.

CHAPTER THREE

Neoliberal Surveillance and Eyes on the Street

In both Regent Park and Lawrence Heights, planning documents emphasize how the spatial layout of the neighborhoods will be redesigned to promote safety and encourage spaces where surveillance is a natural function of everyday activity. In Lawrence Heights, Toronto Community Housing Corporation (TCHC) critiqued "1950s community planning that—though well intentioned—contributes to social and safety issues."[1] The revitalization plan pointed to the importance of mid-rise apartment buildings that "contribute to good public spaces by placing activity and people around the spaces. The height of the buildings helps to facilitate surveillance to help make these spaces safe."[2] Similarly, the *Regent Park Revitalization Study* highlighted how the revitalization of the neighborhood would allow for "eyes on the street'" to increase surveillance: "The built form of the neighborhood will act as a container of public open space, enclosing streets, highlighting corners, defining parks and providing 'eyes on the street' which increases surveillance and safety with separation between them minimized to maintain continuity both of form and activity."[3]

In the previous chapter, I focused on what is characteristically "Canadian" about the revitalization plan: diversity and multiculturalism. While chapter 2 maps uses of diversity and the invocation of multicultural and neoliberal logics and ideals, in this chapter I will explore how surveillance becomes a tool for policing under the guise of community building and community safety. Building on chapter 2, I argue that norms around surveillance encourage entrepreneurial, participatory *and* self-governing neoliberal subjects that reproduce particular populations as in need of regulation and monitoring; I analyze surveillance as a construction of neoliberal diversity projects that is required for social regulation. In this chapter, I understand the employment of eyes on the street in urban revitalization projects as tethered to the racial and class stigmatization of the neighborhoods. Racial and class stigma justifies surveillance and simultaneously reproduces race and class difference in Lawrence Heights and Regent Park. Chapter 3 zooms in on two different modes of surveillance: normalizing surveillance and negotiated surveillance. I analyze these alternate types of surveillance in order to demonstrate the differing modes of social regulation that materialize in efforts to produce and police belonging and exclusion in Regent Park and Lawrence Heights. The everyday surveillance promoted in revitalization positions residents as active participants in the making of neoliberal national identity—being surveilled and surveilling others is described as an essential way to participate and contribute to Canadianness via community building, especially for immigrant and nonwhite residents.

The revitalization plans establish the relationship between security and residents through persistent reference to producing "community," a key marker of Canadian national identity. I investigate how surveillance through "eyes on the street" is tied to the making of a national security state at the most minute level by encouraging residents to monitor their neighbors and embedding this logic in the material plans and design. Surveillance has a long history of attachment to the nation—policing and militias, for example, are isomorphic emblems of the nation and positioned as necessary to protect the nation-state. In both cases, ordinary citizens are called to duty (or nominate themselves, as did George Zimmerman when he murdered Trayvon Martin). Writing about Los Angeles, Mike Davis has analyzed the links among the state, military, and formations of the nation through what he calls the "militarization of space."[4] The "war on poverty" and "war on drugs" in the United States target urban areas—such military metaphors and other references to urban war zones frame cities as key sites for military action and the enforcement of national security. Yet, as Stephen Graham argues, the city has long been a crucial place for the exertion of military ideology and the organization of space around military concerns.[5] Graham cites an article published by former Army Lieutenant Colonel Ralph Peters that describes the need for increased security in cities because "the future of warfare lies in the streets, sewers, high-rise buildings, industrial parks, and the sprawl of houses, shacks, and shelters that form the broken cities of our world."[6] The case of suburbanization during the cold war in response to nuclear threats is an example of the impacts of a military ideology on space.

Surveillance ideologies have given birth to different tactics and strategies to manage populations. On a local level, neighborhood watch programs exemplify community policing that is often endorsed alongside efforts to promote the impact of the built environment on policing and crime.[7] Progressive urban theorist Jane Jacobs promoted the notion of "eyes on the street" to describe the need for better public safety in cities: "There must be eyes on the street, eyes belonging to those we might call the natural proprietors of the street. The buildings on a street equipped to handle strangers and to insure the safety of both residents and strangers, must be oriented to the street.

They cannot turn their backs on blank sides on it and leave it blind . . . The sidewalk must have users on it fairly continuously, both to add to the number of effective eyes on the street and to induce a sufficient number of people in buildings along the street to watch the sidewalks."[8] Jacobs's call for eyes on the street or "natural" surveillance has left a profound legacy in urban studies and planning. Her theorizing of eyes on the street emphasized street level placement of windows in building design to increase the visibility of the street. This type of surveillance, however, is not only tied to the production of a neighborhood or sense of community, rather, "For Jacobs, proximate *watchfulness* is the most rudimentary technology of citizenship. According to this view, despite the ethnic and economic diversity that constitutes urban America, *everyone* can get behind a safe street. As they do so, they become well-rehearsed for formal participation in other seminal institutions of civic life. In point of fact, Jacobs claims that without this basis of watchfulness and casual intimacy among proximate familiars, such institutions will fail."[9] Eyes on the street is an opportunity to practice civic participation in the most mundane of ways. It is an ordinary behavior that acts as a technology to produce and manage populations: a technology that teaches individuals to be "good" community members while simultaneously producing communities that are in need of policing and that should police and watch each other.

Jacobs's concept is closely linked to Crime Prevention through Environmental Design, or CPTED—another urban design strategy or technique of population management and social regulation. Eyes on the street and CPTED are concepts explicitly and implicitly referenced in the revitalization planning documents.[10] The CPTED movement draws connections between the physical environment and crime prevention and informs Oscar Newman's theory of defensible space.[11] Newman's theory is motivated by a study of crime rates in low-rise and high-rise residential buildings in New York City. Newman concluded that rates of crime were higher in high-rise buildings because residents felt no attachment or responsibility in the higher-density and tall buildings. The notion of defensible space has informed urban planning around the world where safety and crime prevention are increased through the design of buildings and the planning of cityscapes. In Regent Park and Lawrence Heights, planners and residents alike casually referenced the role of popular planning trends on material design and security such as CPTED.[12]

In this chapter, I argue that public housing residents in Regent Park and Lawrence Heights are *differentially incorporated* into Canadianness via these community security practices. In the case of revitalization and eyes on the street, surveillance is woven into planning documents and everyday life, naturalizing security practices to affirm values around inclusivity, therefore obscuring everyday realities of exclusion, policing, and racial profiling. Surveillance emerges in ways that properly integrate cultural difference and neoliberal ideology. Therefore, if residents can learn how to behave and to police one another via eyes on the street, they can signal an allegiance to these central characteristics of Canadian national identity. In the following section, I explore eyes on the street and conceptions of safety in the planning documents and from the perspective of residents.

Racialized Surveillance in Canada

While liberal calls for diversity broadcast the success of multiculturalism, analyses of anti-Blackness and police brutality in Canada shine light on how racism operates and impacts daily life. Many scholars have researched the effects of racial profiling on young Black and Latino men and trans folks in particular.[13] Robyn Maynard's extensive research in *Policing Black Lives: State Violence in Canada from Slavery to the Present* carefully maps the historical context of settler colonial racial logics that inform contemporary anti-Black racism in Canada.[14] Her critique of Canadian liberalism underscores how multiculturalism is a mask that disguises the daily surveillance and management of Black Canadians and immigrants, often with deadly consequences. She writes, "On the surface, an official multiculturalism policy enshrined in law, along with the *Charter of Rights and Freedoms*, appears to counter past forms of state-based discrimination. This appearance of equality, however, relies on the erasure of the conditions of Black life in Canada's recent past, as well as its present. For most Black people residing in Canada, neither racial equity, nor "inclusion" or "liberty," to use Justin Trudeau's words, have been achieved. Instead, the realities of ongoing Black subjection only remain more hidden from view."[15] Maynard details the tragic 2003 death of Chevranna Abdi as a deadly example of the limits of inclusion in Canada. Abdi, a trans Black woman, was reported to police by a neighbor—an act of surveillance that ultimately led to Abdi's death while in police custody in Hamilton, Ontario, a small city located southwest of Toronto.[16] The hyperpersecution and policing of trans Black people has received increased attention as a result of organizing efforts that highlight the high rates of violence experienced at the hands of the state. Black Lives Matter Canada's work, built on decades of organizing against racism in Canada, foregrounds the systemic nature of police violence in relation to the surveillance of Black Canadians. This includes the 2014 murder of Jermaine Carby in Toronto and the 2015 murder of Andrew Loku in Ottawa. While Canada often distances itself from the racism and police brutality in the United States, these names, stories, and lives cut short serve as a reminder that Canada is not immune from racism because of multiculturalism and liberal calls for diversity and inclusion. Rather, state surveillance and policing go hand in hand with Canadian neoliberal multiculturalism.

Normalizing Surveillance

> Safety and security are key issues raised by residents in Regent Park and surrounding communities throughout the planning process. Determined by a complex mix of factors, including design characteristics and social issues, planning for community safety requires a range of policies, plans, and partnerships.
>
> —REGENT PARK COLLABORATIVE TEAM, *Regent Park Revitalization Study*, 44

Eyes on the street, CPTED, Neighborhood Watch, and other such forms of surveillance are based on a logic of increased security that transfers policing and surveillance down to the level of the individual. Premised on the idea that *certain* communities need increased policing and surveillance, these forms of surveillance must be compatible with state regulated strategies and techniques (via the military and prison industrial complex). Under a rationale that privileges the security state, there is *recognition* of crime and criminality and a presumption that policing and surveillance are the proven solutions. In revitalization, the surveillance technologies that promote "eyes on the street" adopt a subcontracting of policing, recruiting residents to partake in surveillance; engagement in policing is facilitated through the material design of the neighborhood. The subcontracting of policing to the level of the individual and the role of design are normalized in the planning documents and revitalization. Eyes on the street is normalized by suggesting it will create a safer community, describing the prevalence of crime and employing language around community cohesion and integration. I characterize this set of practices as "normalizing surveillance."

The *Regent Park Social Development Plan* cites academic literature to reinforce the constructed links among surveillance, behavior, safety, and space:

> In other examples, authors point out that feelings of safety are related to "civilities." People who perceive fewer incivilities (for example, graffiti, garbage or broken windows) on their property have a lower fear of crime and a higher sense of their ability to have a positive effect

on their surroundings. They also tend to be more attached to their neighborhood (Brown et al. 2005). In their extensive research on neighborhood cohesion in Chicago, Robert Sampson and Felton Earls (Sampson et al. 1999) found that this phenomenon affected people from all income groups, both homeowners and renters, and that although minor variations occurred across ethno-cultural groups, all groups responded favorably to a reduction of incivilities. . . . The attractiveness of the neighborhood is a significant factor in the perception of comfort and safety.[17]

The logic around perceived incivilities—and that artwork or a lack of trash pickup contribute to incivility or attractiveness—exemplifies the underpinning logic about who is civilized and who is not. This framing also does not attend to the structural conditions at play that move us beyond attributing the impacts of disinvestment to low-income peoples. The connections between safety, behavior, and space are plentiful and can be traced in documents and interviews with planners. In the *Regent Park Revitalization Study*, the authors note, "The [prior] design of the development and the individual buildings has increased the sense of isolation in the neighborhood and created spaces for crime and violence."[18] The planning documents in both neighborhoods assert that revitalization should explicitly address the links between space and safety. Nick, a City of Toronto planner who worked on the revitalization plans in both communities, noted in an interview, "The spaces need to be designed in a way that people who inhabit that space can apply their well-ingrained codes of behavior of how those spaces work. And, when we create spaces that don't let people do that, that is when you start to get problems of crime and other anti-social activities."[19] Nick's phrasing of "well-ingrained codes of behavior" aligns with the logics of CPTED and eyes on the street. However, what is missing from the assertions about the relationship between codes of behavior and the material design of spaces is an analysis about an assumption around the perceived behaviors and how low-income public housing projects and communities of color are hyperpoliced. The emphasis on material design does not consider an analysis of the racialization of space, the spatialization of race, and how perception and racism inform what behaviors are acceptable in what spaces, and by whom, as is evidenced by the brutal murder of Trayvon Martin, who was walking down a well-lit street with a bag of skittles. More precisely, the material design of spaces does not address racist policing practices that violently target communities racialized as nonwhite. No "well-engrained code of behavior" on behalf of residents prevents racial profiling as evidenced by the high rates of carding Black men in Toronto (a widely criticized practice used by the Toronto police that allowed officers to stop people on the street and ask for identification). The social media hashtags #drivingwhileBlack, #shopping whileBlack, and #birdwatchingwhileBlack illuminate how seemingly mundane behaviors are hyperpoliced by both police and white bystanders who perceive the very existence of Black people as a crime. Moreover, the subjective nature of perception embedded in CPTED and eyes on the street makes assumptions about what neighborhoods and spaces are characterized as in need of surveillance technologies. According to an analysis of available crime data on Regent Park, planner and scholar Laura Johnson and historian Robert Johnson argue, "Despite popular belief, Regent seems no more crime-ridden than many other sections of Toronto."[20] The constructed need for surveillance and policing are therefore not because of behaviors per se, but in response to the presence of low-income people of color in a neighborhood.

The Lawrence-Allen Secondary Plan asserts, "New development will have strong regard for the enhancement of community and personal safety by providing casual overlook from development to public spaces and by including building entrances, appropriate active ground floor uses, and transparent building matters along edges of public spaces."[21] Participating in surveillance is portrayed as a way to produce a stronger community—this type of participation constructs surveillance as a national identity building mechanism: by normalizing surveillance while simultaneously celebrating community, security is easily mobilized as a way to participate in common policing practices that are associated with the state security apparatus. The language of "enhancement of community and personal safety" aligns individualized surveillance practices (policing your neighbor) with the language of community. Additionally, "casual overlook" encourages mundane and minute policing to reinforce the "codes of behavior" encouraged by planners. The emphasis on entrances, *appropriate* ground floor uses, and windows or transparent building materials that allow for eyes on the street are all mechanisms that normalize surveillance in efforts to align everyday policing with the building of community. Surveillance is framed as a tool in community building because it provides an opportunity for residents to be engaged and contribute to their neighborhoods—albeit in the form of monitoring their neighbors.

The terms safety, violence, crime, and eyes on the street recur throughout the planning documents and interviews. For example, as described in chapter 1, four themes are highlighted in the *Lawrence-Allen Revitalization*

Plan: reinvestment, mobility, place-making, and livability. While each theme relates to safety and security in Lawrence Heights, place-making specifically focuses on the production of place as a way to "promote public safety."[22] Concerns around safety are also addressed in the *Lawrence-Allen Revitalization Plan* under the theme of "livability." The plan suggested that many areas in the community are "hidden from surveillance by the surrounding roads and the rest of the community," creating the risk of crime and violence.[23] In a research paper on Lawrence Heights, architect Mark Sterling and TCHC manager Lorne Cappe asserted, "A deteriorated building stock combined with social, physical, and income isolation has led to problems such as youth gangs and violent crime. However, the largely immigrant population has a strong sense of community. Yet, despite isolation, Lawrence Heights residents are understood as having a "strong sense of community."[24] Here, Sterling and Cappe rely on key tropes of Canadian multiculturalism and national identity in their reference to the "immigrant population" and "community" in their commentary about the relationship between the built environment and crime. These discursive alignments reinforce the racial stigmatization of Lawrence Heights in relation to the ideals of Canadian multiculturalism.

Similarly, the *Regent Park Secondary Plan* describes cultural diversity as a strength of the community but criticizes the poor planning because it "facilitates criminal activity":

> Regent Park was initially successful in that it provided quality, new housing to many low-income residents. As the neighborhood evolved, it developed many strengths, including cultural diversity and a strong sense of community among its residents. At the same time, challenges have emerged. The housing stock has deteriorated and no longer provides quality housing. The buildings in Regent Park have a poor relationship to the surrounding open spaces. Public spaces are often poorly designed and many residents have found that the design *facilitates criminal activity and undermines public safety* [emphasis added]. The neighborhood has become both physically and socially isolated from the surrounding areas and the rest of Toronto.[25]

Like Sterling and Cappe's reflections about Lawrence Heights, crime and isolation have affected Regent Park, and the documents highlighted how the built environment contributed to increased crime and violence.[26] Nick reiterated the importance of planning in facilitating safety, echoing the logic of CPTED: "Spaces need to be surrounded by streets and buildings that are active and well used, because when people are around, when they are taking their kids to the park to play, when they are walking their dog, when they are walking down the street, when they are driving down the street, those create surveillance of those spaces, and just by virtue of all of the activity that is happening there, and then when those spaces are safe, people will interact with each other and form strong community bonds."[27] For Nick, surveillance is a part of everyday life leading to an interactive engagement between community members that produces stronger community bonds and echoes Jane Jacobs's call for security at the most minute levels.[28]

Additionally, the plans highlight residents' concerns about safety that are linked to security specifically through the promotion of "eyes on the street" alongside the technology of diversity: "It would improve safety through more 'eyes on the street' and provide opportunities for the community to celebrate and share its diverse cultures."[29] In this instance, surveillance is framed to produce opportunities for the community to celebrate the cultural diversity of the neighborhood, linking cultural diversity (a primary signifier of "Canadianness") and surveillance. Normalized surveillance is promoted via eyes on the street in relation to cultural diversity. This seemingly random positioning of diversity alongside safety aligns diversity and surveillance as tools of neoliberal multiculturalism.

The ties between cultural diversity and surveillance are not straightforward. In some cases, diversity is a challenge to be managed, while in other instances diversity alongside revitalization is a resource that can help *create* community. The shift from diversity as a problem to a resource makes diversity align with social management techniques like surveillance and eyes on the street. This type of participatory and individualized surveillance hinges on the reality that certain residents are unevenly surveilled *because* of their perceived cultural diversity, where culture easily stands in for racial and class difference and disparity. The diversity of incomes, as explored in chapter 2, is framed as a way to promote "codes of behavior" and supports a logic in which low-income residents are produced as in need of policing and surveillance. Furthermore, multiculturalism is a regulating technology because it positions those deemed culturally different as manageable under a multicultural framework.

Chapter 2 examined the logic in the plan that suggests new middle-income residents would help to decrease crime in the neighborhood. A diversity of income aligns with surveillance technologies by asserting that higher income residents will "enforce stricter ground rules": "Behavioural patterns of lower-income tenants will be altered by interaction with higher-income neighbours. . . . The crime rate will fall as high-income residents enforce stricter ground rules for the community."[30] There is an explicit assertion about the moral superiority of middle-income residents who can influence the perceived criminal behavior of residents who live in subsidized units. This racist and classist logic is rooted in assumptions about the moral high-ground of middle- and high-income residents.

In summary, the employment of the technology of eyes on the street in the revitalizations relies on emphasis of cohesion, community, and integration—all core values of Canadianness emphasized in multiculturalism policy and practice in Canada.[31] Normalized surveillance reinscribes the production of residents as in need of everyday monitoring because of their constructed otherness and the perceived "suspicious" behavior of stigmatized populations. Finally, building on chapter 2, normalized surveillance recruits the rhetoric(s) of neoliberal multiculturalism: not only are individuality and self-regulation valued, but such practices will actually also allow for a celebration of the diverse cultures in the community. Here, diversity is once again a marker of disparity and legitimizes the policing of residents. For residents, such practices are not simply imposed and accepted.

Negotiated Surveillance

> VANESSA: A lot of people say that with revitalization, Regent Park
>   will be a safer place. What do you think about that?
> AMEENA: I never felt that unsafe in Regent Park.
> —Interview with Ameena, December 20, 2010

The planning documents that reported the findings from community consultation sessions highlighted safety concerns, as well as residents' support for increased security. Yet, in interviews residents offered a more nuanced understanding of security and safety and discussed varying conceptions of community. While residents did not have a homogenous voice and unified position (something I explore in chapter 4), there was a distinct difference between resident perspectives and the narratives in the planning documents and by planners. This section examines these varying resident perspectives on safety and security and focuses on three different ways that residents made sense of security efforts: 1) a critique of the mixed-income model as a community safety strategy; 2) formations of community in relation to crime, not despite crime; and 3) community as an untapped resource. In each of these three ways, residents formulate alternative visions of community that exist outside of the boundaries of the revitalization framework. I label this negotiated surveillance to reflect the ways that residents both critiqued the revitalizations' surveillance frameworks and normalized surveillance, but also because in some cases residents engaged with and reconciled the need for community safety strategies and wanted to promote a safe and vibrant neighborhood.

Negotiating Class: Surveillance and the Mixed-Income Framework

In Regent Park, Greg, a community activist, addressed the links between re-vitalization and crime.[32] Greg outlined how Regent Park was portrayed as isolated because of the violence in the community. However, he highlighted the emphasis placed on the new middle-class residents and their perceptions of crime. He speculated the middle-class residents that moved into Regent Park would call the police more often than former Regent Park residents for issues that do not necessarily require police attention (an assertion that cannot be confirmed due to limited neighborhood level policing data). Greg acknowledged the role of "through streets" (e.g., streets that pass all the way through the community as opposed to the previous streets that were blocked by cul-de-sacs and cut off the neighborhood, a planning strategy that was criticized in the mid-twentieth century construction of public housing) and new buildings to reduce crime, but he did not assume that violence and crime will disappear. In fact, at several points in the interview, he made the argument that crime and drug dealing were not unique to Regent Park. He remarked that drug use was rampant in Toronto's wealthiest neighborhoods (e.g., Forest Hill and Rosedale), but that it is "behind closed doors." For Greg, because of the class status of these neighborhoods, the residents and their drug use are not stigmatized or criminalized in the same way as residents in public housing.

Greg argued that there is a difference in response to crime based on class status. He described the class differences in two ways. First, he asserted that new middle-income residents will call the police, even for activity that does not warrant police involvement. Similarly, he highlighted the stigmatized nature of crime in Regent Park despite the fact that similar crime happens in middle- and upper-income neighborhoods. Second, Greg agreed with the planning of through streets and new buildings as these strategies are linked to crime prevention. However, Greg contextualized crime prevention and the relationship between occurrences and perceptions of crime by pointing out again that crime "is all over." His critique challenged the constructed discourse about the isolated nature of crime and violence in Regent

Park and Lawrence Heights (especially asserted by the media), and also challenged the idea that the presence of the new middle-class residents would increase safety. While Greg's critique focused on class boundaries, it must also be read in relation to scholarship that highlights the overpolicing of historically racially segregated neighborhoods.[33]

Community worker and former Regent Park resident Chandra questioned the widespread notion that there is a connection between income and the incidence of crime.[34] Her comments point to how behavior was a direct concern of the planners because revitalization was thought to influence the behavior of residents in Regent Park through CPTED and eyes on the street. In particular, Chandra spoke to the logic of integration explored in chapter 2, whereby middle-income residents influence the behavior of low-income residents (e.g., middle-income residents as role models). The logic insists that both the built environment and the encouragement of policing your neighbors increase safety, but also that eventually crime will decrease because of a shift in individual behavior due to the positive impact of middle-income residents. Chandra and Greg firmly challenged the view that crime is a result of psychological tendencies that can be addressed by the proximity of "good" middle-class role models.

Resident critiques of the mixed-income framework challenge normalized surveillance, which presumes that crime and a lack of safety is tied to both individualized and psychologized tendencies or behaviors that are not correlated with structural or systemic causes (hence the argument that providing good role models in the form of middle-class residents can reshape behavior). Residents, however, saw crime as related to a lack of resources and the stigma attached to the community. There was a sense of the propensity to overdiagnose crime in TCHC neighborhoods, while ignoring it in whiter, wealthier neighborhoods.

Community Formation and Crime

Resident responses to questions about crime and violence inspired conversations about these issues in their everyday lives. While ideas about policing, eyes on the street, and CPTED further regulate the communities by increasing surveillance, community responses were much more pragmatic. For example, Eva told me, "You know, you see everything here. My kids seen it all. Yeah, it's sad, my kids seen it, when the drug dealers were doing their pipes in the stairways and sniffing their stuff, burning cocaine on a spoon and all that. They have seen it all. Shooting, everything. But how can you prevent that? All I try to teach my children is don't hang around with them. Mind your own business. . . . You have to know how to live and survive."[35] Another Regent Park resident, Sheila, who was relocated to a TCHC neighborhood across the city, similarly characterized how violence affects her family. Sheila described to me the sound of hearing gunshots one evening: "Like I said, we've lived in Regent and we know exactly what is going on so we can tell a gunshot from a firecracker now."[36] For Sheila and her children, she gained a sense of awareness about violence, crime, and drug use during her time in Regent Park. There was little denial among residents that there was violence and crime in their communities. Yet, alongside this acknowledgement of the daily realities of crime, most residents defended the sense of community, the strong community bonds, and the community's desire to stop the violence. While Sheila and Eva addressed their everyday encounters with violence, they also consistently reminded me about the unique community in Regent Park. Eva noted, "I feel more safe here than everywhere else. I know the people in the community."[37] In Regent Park, Sheila also called into question the constructed ideas about safety and violence by highlighting the relationships that perceived "criminals" maintained with their neighbors: "Like even though those big guys were doing drugs and everything, they were very good for the kids. They were watchful for the kids, they looked out for the kids and everything."[38] Sheila's perspective must also be contextualized because she was displaced by the revitalization. She was relocated to a TCHC community in the west end of the city. In the interview, she highlighted the fact that there was crime and violence, like in any neighborhood, but because Regent Park was a tight knit community, she did not fear for the safety of her children. In fact, Sheila trusted her neighbors would provide safety and security for her family and neighborhood. For this reason, Sheila was frustrated by her displacement and wanted to return to Regent Park to be reconnected with her neighbors and friends.[39]

Aliyyah, a young mother of a five-year-old daughter who lived in Neptune, the TCHC neighborhood adjacent to Lawrence Heights, was hired to engage residents in the consultation process (explored in chapter 4).[40] She highlighted the economic dynamics of the community and the isolation experienced by young people who turn to selling drugs to financially support themselves.[41] Like Sheila and Eva, Aliyyah challenged the stigma that was attached to the neighborhoods and had a much more layered critique of crime and the need for increased surveillance in Regent Park and Lawrence Heights. Aliyyah also identified the structural causes of poverty and the lack of resources provided to youth in Lawrence Heights and Neptune.

Furthermore, one of the key themes highlighted by Eva, Sheila, and Aliyyah was that their main concern was not about the presence of drug use or criminals but whether or not their children were safe. They did not see their children's safety and crime in opposition to each other (e.g., that because of their children seeing people use drugs that they would not be safe). Rather, each of these women's perspectives and various critiques of structural inequality demonstrates the ways in which they negotiated their everyday realities.

Through negotiated surveillance, residents opt out of eyes on the street and normalized surveillance. In the case of the latter, described in Sheila's and Eva's interviews, where police are seen as using heavy-handed tactics to "keep the community safe," residents offered critiques and included "criminals" as community members. Moreover, residents challenged two normalized discourses in relation to crime: that residents want cops to come in and "clean up" Regent Park and Lawrence Heights and the notion that there are ideal communities (Greg's reference to Rosedale). Overall, their perspectives highlight how the approaches to crime reduction and surveillance were simply not practical. These residents felt they were part of a strong and close-knit community and did not view a mixing of incomes as the solution to crime. In fact, they challenged the very premise that their neighborhood needed eyes on the street or increased surveillance at all.

Community as an Untapped Resource

The three characteristics of negotiated surveillance—a critique of mixed-income housing, the relationship between constructions of crime and community, and community as a resource—all offer a glimpse into the complexities of conceptions of community for residents. In planning documents and interviews, no single or coherent definition of community exists despite the communitarian language of social cohesion that emerges in the plans. The top-down construction of community stands in stark contrast from residents' understanding of community as an untapped resource. The planning documents generally characterize ideas about community cohesiveness in terms of cultural diversity and integration; crime and violence, on the other hand, are features of the neighborhood that stand in opposition to the ideals of community that the revitalization strives to support and produce. Residents, however, characterized their communities as vibrant and understand crime and violence primarily in relation to police discrimination and profiling.

Tamia, a Lawrence Heights resident involved with the revitalization process, critiqued police engagement with residents in Lawrence Heights:

"When the police come in, they come in with ideas in the back of their head so when they are dealing with people, they are not dealing with people like people. . . . We are animals because we are from the jungle, right."[42] Tamia's account questions how police encounters with residents are shaped by ideas about the community as being the "jungle," the neighborhood's nickname, signifying the violent, chaotic, and animalistic racist stereotypes attached to Lawrence Heights that seemingly oppose language around inclusion and community. Such encounters simultaneously produce residents as in need of policing. These stereotypes and stigmas are mobilized to justify racial profiling and violence.[43] Tamia challenged this view by questioning the ways that the police treat residents and reinforce negative stereotypes of a violent and criminal community. For example, Tamia emphasized the close-knit nature of Lawrence Heights: "It is a fun, close-knit community, you know. People tend to know [other] people. Like the environment, it is nice. It is friendly. It is warm. . . . It feels like a community. When I go outside of Lawrence Heights it feels like I am foreign. . . . The people here are good. It is close knit. And I like the greenery. It is the jungle. You know it is funny because it has a negative connotation but to me the jungle is a positive thing."[44] Tamia identified Lawrence Heights as her home; she goes so far as to say she feels "foreign" outside of Lawrence Heights, identifying an allegiance and shared identity with her neighbors who live within the boundaries of the Jungle. Here, foreign also signals national boundaries and belonging as a term associated with people who are not from "here" or are foreign to Canada. Tamia's comments, among the other interviewees, are an example of negotiated surveillance: by articulating their understandings of community in contrast to that of planners and police, residents call into question the attempt to reinforce the *norms* of the security state in their neighborhood.

Responding to the idea that revitalization could address crime and violence, Tamia said, "The community is always going to be a community. It is how it is branded. People have this notion right now that this is the hood. . . . I think things are still going to happen. I don't think it is going to change. . . . I don't think it will make a bit of a difference."[45] Tamia noted a disjuncture between her perspective as a resident and the planners' pledge to increase security through the revitalization. In our interview, Tamia described the profiling and the stigmatization of the community, calling into question the extent to which crime and violence are "inherent" in the neighborhood. Instead, she highlighted the "branding" and reputation of Lawrence Heights and how these are tied to stigma. Tamia argued that addressing heightened security with cameras without placing "worth" on the neighborhood will not increase security but instead will maintain the status quo marginalization of the neighborhood. The production of the neighborhood as a ghetto and a "jungle" by police exists in relation to racialized violence and the militarization of urban space through security apparatuses, which legitimizes the profiling of and violence against Black and Brown people.[46]

As Chandra, a former Regent Park resident and community advocate argued,

> We have been painted like these poor, downtrodden people,
> you know. So that has kind of bothered me throughout this whole
> [process]. . . . What can we do for those poor people over there? Well
> we are not! We are not! I say there is a lot to be learned from the people
> who have come to live here in Regent Park. What they have been
> through, lived in countries where there have been no government
> supports and no way, means, and what have you, and they come here
> and have a lot to offer Canadian people about you know, community,
> development, capacity building, fortitude, resilience; it [the commu-
> nity] is an untapped resource. But painted with this picture, a small
> group of young people will get in trouble with the law and it paints the
> whole population. What about the 95 percent that are successful? And
> I feel that way about our community. We have been sold off as this,
> you know, group of people who needs to be fixed. Our community
> didn't need to be fixed. It needed to be resourced.[47]

Fixing the community through revitalization simultaneously involves criminalizing Regent Park and its residents. By using the phrasing "Canadian people," Chandra signals the ways that residents are actually distanced from a normative construction of Canadian identity. Cultural diversity, then, is not much of a value but a way to construct residents as outsiders in need of fixing and management. Chandra challenged the notion of "fixing Regent Park" to highlight the vibrancy of the community. When Chandra described the different resources in the community, she pointed to what the community has to offer to "Canadian people." The language she embraces, "community, development, capacity building, fortitude, resilience," contrasts the call for "eyes on the street" and the minute policing of one's neighbors. More importantly, Chandra highlighted how resident engagement and response simultaneously *polices* the revitalization process and defines community on their own terms. Therefore, the planners' construction of safety and security through design produces a counter effect—the comments of community members problematize normalized surveillance and call into question the power relations that shape the revitalization and notions of "surveillance."

While the production of normalizing surveillance is encouraged by the promotion of eyes on the street in the revitalization plans, I argue that residents insisted upon differing nuanced conceptions of community and safety that challenge the plan's promotion of surveillance. Chandra's questioning of the mixing of incomes and Tamia's emphasis on how the community is viewed by those who do not live in Lawrence Heights (as opposed to her experiences as part of a vibrant community) are examples of negotiated surveillance. In both cases, it is not that residents rejected the idea of safety. Rather, residents rejected the logic of eyes on the street that is based on a construction of racialized and stigmatized stereotypes about their communities that do not challenge the status quo, racial profiling, or socioeconomic inequality. Instead, by naming the assumptions about the links between class and crime, residents openly critiqued the normalization of policing.

In sum, residents challenged the idea that eyes on the street via revitalization would make the community safer. Eva and Sheila articulated that despite their encounters with violence they never felt unsafe. In fact, Eva noted she felt unsafe and threatened around the police, not residents. Tamia similarly argued that there might be crime and violence, but the level of crime would not change because of normalizing surveillance; instead, what is needed is a change of perception among planners and police. Chandra, Greg, and Tamia questioned the idea that the new middle-class residents, in particular, would have a positive effect on the security and safety of the neighborhood. Finally, Chandra threw into sharp relief how much "Canada" has to learn from the residents of Regent Park. Each of these examples highlights different aspects of negotiated surveillance. Residents amplified their perspectives by naming the limits of surveillance and challenged the implication that they were uniquely in need of management via normalized surveillance because of where they live and who they are.

Normalized and Negotiated Encounters

A community meeting held by the Toronto police to solicit support from residents highlighted the tenuous terrain between negotiated and normalizing surveillance. The community meeting was held on November 4, 2010, at the Regent Park Community Center from 6 to 9 P.M. Approximately seventy-five people were in attendance. The meeting was facilitated by the local councilor,

Pam McConnell, and consisted of six presentations by the local police division 51 and TCHC representatives.[48] The meeting was called after several months of heightened violence and three murders in the neighborhood.

One of the presentations focused on the most recent murder in Regent Park that took place barely a week earlier at approximately 3:00 A.M. on Monday, October 25. Twenty-four-year-old Albert Kiwubeyi, a young Black man, was gunned down at close range on the corner of Sackville and Shuter streets. He was found at 3:03 A.M. on the sidewalk. Kiwubeyi was enrolled in school and worked for the Kiwanis Club in Regent Park. His family lived in Regent Park but were relocated as part of the revitalization process. This was the third murder in the neighborhood in October 2010. Sealand White, 15, and Jermaine Derby, 19, both Black, were shot to death on October 9 at Whiteside Place in Regent Park.

The presentation focused on the details of the murder and a request from police for help from the community. The police repeatedly stated that one of the major problems in Regent Park was that residents do not help police by coming forward with information, a direct appeal to discourses of normalizing surveillance. Several times during the meeting, the police solicited help from residents and alluded to residents' responsibility to make their own communities safer. Race was an undercurrent of the conversation but was never directly mentioned. It is worth noting that not only were all of the deaths that were talked about Black men, but white men and women led the meeting with an audience of primarily nonwhite community members.

Following the presentation on Albert Kiwubeyi's death, there were two other presentations about increased policing in Regent Park. Several initiatives were being developed to increase security. For example, ten police officers would be assigned to Regent Park to "walk the beat" from 7:00 P.M. until 2:00 A.M., as well as an increase in the presence of undercover officers. Also, a new Regent Park hotline was going to be established to encourage residents to give anonymous tips. The police described these efforts as part of a "genuine" attempt at community development and relationship building between police and residents.

The meeting ended with a question and answer period. While the meeting was organized to discuss the increasing violence, there were several comments made about the state of housing in Regent Park and its connection to the violence. Two comments specifically addressed lighting and lighting's impact on community safety. Residents asked why the lights were broken all of the time and complained about the long response time from TCHC to repair broken lights. A TCHC representative responded by saying that they fix the lights every two days, but residents kept breaking them. Parents expressed a concern about the fact that it was not safe for children to walk home after school and that they were not able to participate in activities like trick-or-treating on Halloween—an interesting contrast to the safety and sense of community identified by several interviewees. One resident emphasized that this was not always the case in Regent Park and was a very recent phenomenon. Residents reminisced about the East Coast blackout of 2003 where they described how the community came together despite the lack of lighting. One person even argued that people from other TCHC neighborhoods wanted to be in Regent Park during that time because of how close-knit the neighborhood was and celebrated the sense of community that existed in Regent Park.

During the question and answer period, the revitalization was explicitly mentioned five times. On one occasion, Eva spoke up and claimed that there was increased security around the new buildings and not the rest of Regent Park; she expressed anger that the new condos had twenty-four-hour security and the rest of the neighborhood did not. TCHC refuted Eva's remarks and repeatedly stated that Eva's claim around uneven security was not true. The market-rate condos in Regent Park do have twenty-four-hour front desk attendants. The interaction between Eva and the residents who addressed concerns about lighting was a signal of the overall distrust between residents and TCHC. This example showcases the perception among some residents that the new residents in the condos have twenty-four-hour security. Many TCHC residents' comments at the meeting and in interviews made it clear that they associate normalized surveillance and safety measures with class privilege. Further, Eva's point was not that the rent-geared-to-income (RGI) buildings should also have twenty-four-hour security. Instead, she highlighted two problems. First, she pointed out that the market buildings were perceived to have different resources than the other buildings, which exposed a disparity between market and RGI units. Second, her comment underscored the stigma attached to the residents who lived in public housing such that their middle-income neighbors needed twenty-four-hour protection.

The tensions around the revitalization and surveillance were marked in several confrontational interactions during the meeting. In one encounter, a self-identified twenty-two-year-old Black female resident accused the facilitator, Pam McConnell, the long-time white female city councilor, for being "out of touch" with the audience and not giving people a chance to speak. The resident suggested that Councilor McConnell was "talking too much but not saying anything." The same resident also expressed anger at

TCHC because of bullet holes on the exterior walls of the community center. As a resident and community worker, she walked kids home from after-school programs and explained that they had to walk by the bullet holes. She questioned what message the bullet holes in the wall sends to the children. She stated that TCHC intentionally let the buildings deteriorate. She ended by proclaiming that "just because residents are poor does not mean they deserve inadequate housing." This statement alongside Eva's comments signals the resentment among residents about the stigma of Regent Park and the novel value being placed on the community because of the new middle-class residents who moved in during the revitalization, erasing the experience of long-time low-income residents who expressed concerns about the condition of the buildings. The overarching tone of the meeting was one of distrust. Residents expressed a strong distrust of police and explained that they hesitated to come forward with information because they feared retaliation from the accused if they were to report.[49] The issue of distrust and retaliation came up in several interviews with residents who described specific incidents that made them feel like they could not trust the police to honor anonymity if they were to report a crime. Before the meeting ended, a white community worker expressed dissatisfaction with the "patronizing tone of the police presentations" that started the meeting. He stated that he felt like he was in school being talked down to, that the presentations were "talking at residents as opposed to engaging with them as participants." He stated, "This is not how you engage with a community; if police want residents to cooperate, then they have to treat them like humans."[50] The hostility could not be missed—there was explicit conflict between residents and community workers and TCHC, Toronto police, and the city councilor.

The back and forth between residents, police, and TCHC officials underscored the tensions that arise between normalized and negotiated surveillance: while residents accepted (and in some cases demanded) resources to prompt safety, such as better lighting, they rejected the top-down security apparatus that criminalized residents and the neighborhood. From an outside perspective, the community meeting was an opportunity for residents to speak out about the injustices they experienced. They specifically named the role of the city, TCHC, and the police in creating injustice and disparity. Residents who critiqued the councilor, police, and normalized surveillance transformed a meeting on safety and surveillance facilitated by the police. This is negotiated surveillance in the most profound sense. Residents created alternative engagement practices to critique formal notions of surveillance that encouraged residents to police one another and increased police presence in their neighborhood. The interactions at the meeting highlight the multiple ways residents made sense of community safety. There was both a critique of the police and a refusal of imposed normalized surveillance, but there was also a desire for new lighting and other safety measures as long as the approach to safety challenged racist and classist practices that stigmatized and targeted residents and their neighborhood.

Conclusion

The management techniques of eyes on the street and CPTED, strategies of governmentality, are quintessentially neoliberal: the recruitment of residents to patrol one another is a perfect articulation of individual participation alongside Canadian idioms of cultural difference. So, on the one hand, the multicultural "eyes" incorporated in everyday street surveillance of one's neighbors is an inclusive practice. With CPTED and the physical urban design changes, eyes representing various backgrounds are brought together to produce community by bringing these eyes to a common focus. On the other hand, with the superficial inclusion in these individualized policing and surveillance efforts it does not much matter whose eyes are on the street as long as they are participating. In fact, *who* is being watched is of central concern. Lastly, one of the primary tensions that emerges in the planning logics is how eyes on the street and CPTED rely on how Lawrence Heights and Regent Park are constructed and racialized as nonwhite and low-income neighborhoods. As urban studies scholar Parastou Saberi argues in her study of Toronto's perceived "Paris Problem" referencing uprisings in the banlieues of Paris, "As the demographic composition of cities has become more diverse, the figure of the 'immigrant' and their everyday spaces have been demonised, with varying intensities, for being a threat to Canadian 'values,' 'way of life,' social cohesion and democracy, and for causing 'threats' for concentrated poverty, 'gangs and guns,' 'radicalisation,' 'terrorism,' and even the recent rise of hard right populism in Toronto."[51] Saberi highlights the ways the media constructed connections between "immigrant neighborhoods" as oppositional and even as a threat to constructed Canadianness. This logic produces neighborhoods like Regent Park and Lawrence Heights as therefore in need of policing. In the plans' uses of security logics, there is an implicit assumption that residents *require* such forms of policing. The web of logics about immigrants, policing, and Canadian identity operate in the name of community building and celebrating diversity through revitalization. The liberal narrative that shapes normalized surveillance presumes that citizens' individual freedoms help maintain community. The logic insists that in order to preserve these freedoms, citizens should patrol one another's behavior; by patrolling one another's behavior, they construct community and therefore ensure freedom and belonging.

This chapter examined three aspects of surveillance in urban revitalization: 1) how the revitalization of Regent Park and Lawrence Heights employed neoliberal state surveillance logics at the local level; 2) how residents were positioned and understood in relation to the need for "eyes on the street"; and 3) how residents simultaneously understood and defined community, which operates as a critique to eyes on the street and normalized surveillance. As Tamia noted, "I don't see changes unless they (the police) change up their ground. They change how they do things. Learn how to work from a grassroots model. You know. Learn how to do community policing better. Taking away certain stigma they have. Sometimes it is the people 'in there' that need change in order to make it better."[52] Residents of Regent Park and Lawrence Heights, like Tamia and Chandra, offered microinterventions and commentaries as a mode of turning "eyes" onto authority to critique and challenge power and the positioning of residents as in need of surveillance. These interventions are a feature of negotiated surveillance where residents spoke back to top-down narratives about the criminalization of their neighborhoods.

The surveillance of Regent Park and Lawrence Heights attempts to produce community members of a particular kind: a model community member actively participates in surveillance and policing. However, residents simultaneously insisted upon notions of community and safety that do not necessarily correspond with the aims of revitalization and produce a critique of surveillance. When asked about safety and security, residents talked about the strength of the community, the failures of the police, and the lack of resources from the City of Toronto and TCHC. By considering how residents carefully articulated their understandings of community as well as contested ideas about CPTED and eyes on the street, we can see how residents define and create vibrant communities in relation to their everyday experiences, not despite them.

CHAPTER FOUR

Canadians in the Making

Community Engagement and Procedural Participation

For Diana, a City of Toronto planner, engaging with residents was an important part of the revitalization planning process: "We are a diverse city, and I think it is extremely important to engage newcomers. For one, we have a lot to learn from them. And they have a lot to learn on civic engagement and that they actually have a voice in this process. *And kind of teaching them how to be Canadian* [emphasis added]. As a group, you [residents] have a really strong voice and you [residents] can effect change."[1]

While her use of concepts such as diversity, "newcomers," and civic engagement seem like an ordinary alignment in the Canadian landscape of liberal multiculturalism, they reveal a particular ideology about political subjectivity and what it means to be "Canadian." Diana's choice of words is noteworthy because she positions residents' status as newcomers as an opportunity to *teach* them how to be Canadian. For Diana, new immigrants have the opportunity to learn about Canadian civics by participating in the revitalization consultations. In less explicit form, similar notions around multicultural engagement and participation surface throughout the planning documents. If a marker of Canadianness and multiculturalism is to welcome newcomers and include immigrants in Canadian society, then civic engagement and consultations are quintessential opportunities for residents to learn about and embrace these particularly Canadian liberal democratic ideals.

Against the backdrop of chapters 2 and 3, Diana's remarks capture a profound contradiction: residents' difference is constituted through their positioning as culturally other newcomers (read: nonwhite) and therefore *not* Canadian even though a large percentage of residents were in fact Canadian citizens. While 82.5 percent and 85 percent of residents of Regent Park and Lawrence Heights were Canadian citizens prior to revitalization, respectively, both neighborhoods have significant immigrant presence. In Lawrence Heights, 57 percent of the overall population in the neighborhood was made up of immigrants.[2] In Regent Park, 4,000 residents arrived in Canada between 1996 and 2006.[3]

Diana's rhetoric suggests the process and planners can teach newcomers "how to be Canadian" yet circumscribes the type of Canadianness that is available to them. As argued in chapter 2, the ground on which difference is understood presupposes the modes of exclusion. In community consultations, residents were understood and positioned as raced and classed "others" and therefore not Canadian, but they have the potential to become included in Canadianness via revitalization. As I explore in this chapter, however, inclusion efforts are limited because of the very presupposition of difference that shapes the views of authority figures like Diana in regard to consultation and revitalization.

I examine how, while consultations and participation were positioned as symbols of Canadian democracy and inclusion, revitalization both recruited residents to participate in the planning process and simultaneously limited their participation. Although consultations in Regent Park and Lawrence Heights were "community" based, participation was a procedure with little focus on the value or content of participation. The city measured community consultation by individual participation and quantified it as such—planners' and consultants' referenced estimations of how many residents attended meetings or were reached in consultation. However, the content of participation did not much matter as long as individuals were participating (filling out surveys or forms, putting up Post-it notes during consultations, or attending town halls). I call this "procedural participation" to mark the neoliberal articulation and ritualistic modes of engagement in the consultation process.

Despite the limitations of procedural participation, residents created their own meaning in the process through critique and contestation, and sometimes embrace. In some cases, residents challenged the technical practices of the consultations and questioned the process; in other instances, residents felt their participation was meaningful and could be empowering. Those who felt that they had been ignored in the consultations and/or questioned the "promises" made during the planning process often still articulated a desire to participate and build community. Contestation and critique of the consultations led some residents to remain engaged in the revitalization plans whether or not they felt like they would have an impact.

This chapter is organized in three sections. First, I provide an overview of the relationship among development, planning, and participation and engagement on both international and urban scales. Next, I summarize the community consultation process in Regent Park and Lawrence Heights. Then, I examine how procedural participation and critique took shape in the engagement process. The data included focuses on the first three to five years of the revitalization processes in both neighborhoods.

The Project of Participation

Participation serves a key legitimizing function in democratic societies. Participation, often via voting or civic engagement, provides a foundation for democracies, giving citizens an opportunity to debate and make decisions about their societies. Activist groups such as labor and anticolonial movements have long sought participation as a primary feature of mobilization and organization as a tool and strategy for self-organization and the production of alternative social visions.[4] One strand of relevant participatory planning theory and practice has its roots in international development and emphasizes projects in the global south and the involvement of local communities in planning their environments and social worlds, inspired by democratic principles.[5] In the context of development and planning in the global south, participatory development, formally called "participatory reflection and action" (PRA), is based on the idea of "empowering" community members by involving them in the development process/project. It emerged as a critique of top-down neocolonial development policy; PRA frameworks were designed to "empower" marginalized populations that have previously been excluded from political processes.[6] In some cases, the end goal is to "train" the local community to lead project implementation. In other contexts, the community works alongside development agencies or planners as local informants to ensure that the project meets local needs. Participatory planning acknowledges that historically marginalized peoples can and should participate in theorizing and planning their lives and communities.[7] Robert Chambers, a leader of the international development movement, highlighted the importance of *letting* local communities facilitate the process of critical self-reflection by facilitators and participants, and personal responsibility of community members.[8]

In urban planning, related models encouraging participation and engagement have been extensively theorized, promoted, and critiqued.[9] Communicative or collaborative planning is an approach where different community stakeholders are involved in the planning process as opposed to more traditional rational and top-down urban planning models. In a communicative approach, stakeholders work together to develop solutions for different planning issues and often work toward consensus-building. Communicative and collaborative approaches to planning have been critiqued for a lack of consideration of power relations and to trouble the goal of consensus-building.[10] In the context of public housing revitalization, participatory models have been critiqued "because mixed-income communities replacing public housing developments are more contrived—centrally designed and to some extent centrally managed—deliberation and decision making in them are also substantially influenced by development teams and property management, who have a direct role both in 'creating' these new communities and in shaping key inputs that will fundamentally condition neighborhood life."[11] Skeptics therefore question the role of consultations in planning processes because of the power dynamics and roles of developers, planners, and housing authorities. Ultimately, the concern is that those with power and funding make the final decisions.

There is much debate about consultations and participation, as well as the disagreement around the correct conceptual framing of "community."[12] Because of the emphasis on local and community voice, there is a risk of homogenizing communities and approaching the concepts of local and community as "self-evident and unproblematic social categories."[13] Acknowledging the heterogeneity of communities and social spaces can prevent essentialism in participation processes.[14]

Beyond essentialism, skeptics have proposed a broad range of criticisms of participatory projects in development contexts that extend to communicative planning approaches. They have been labeled as tyrannical and authoritarian, legitimizing rule through produced consensus. Bill Cooke and Uma Kothari's edited volume *Participation: The New Tyranny* explores these concerns.[15] Cooke and Kothari criticize the lack of engagement by development actors with how power operates in participatory frameworks. As contributor Harry Taylor points out, participatory discourses provide "the 'sense' and warm emotional pull of participation without its substance, and thus [are] an attempt to placate those without power and obscure the real levers of power inherent in the social relations of global capitalism."[16] Taylor argues that practitioners feel emotionally committed to these frameworks but that they do not create space for actually engaging disadvantaged groups. PRA is invested in the empowerment of local communities in making decisions about governance and is thought to bring democratic practices to contexts where communities have been excluded from participation and decision-making. In the context of this chapter, PRA is relevant not only because of the participatory models used in the revitalization frameworks but because participation is a core feature of democracy and the construction of Canada is an inclusive multicultural democratic society. As the word "inclusive" implies, all residents are encouraged to engage in decision-making processes.

Engagement in the Revitalization of Regent Park and Lawrence Heights

While the Ontario Planning Act mandates at least one public meeting where people can voice opinions and concerns for specific development projects, consultation and community engagement included many meetings, consultations, and forums in Regent Park and Lawrence Heights.[17] The planning process in both Regent Park and Lawrence Heights included various engagement efforts, such as meetings, town halls, and community outreach, via selected community representatives known as community animators, encouraging different forms of participation. Toronto Community Housing Corporation (TCHC) lists the Regent Park planning principles on its website; the fourth is "Involve the community in the process." According to the *Regent Park Community Engagement Team Report*, "The Regent Park process was a visibly inclusive, community oriented process focused on revitalizing a community widely known for its troubles (and less widely known for its successes). The positive response from within the community was encouraging."[18] The revitalization study also emphasized resident engagement and claims the community would be involved in each step of the process.[19] It described a methodology for the consultations created by an outside agency, Public Interest Strategy & Communications, in collaboration with an independent development consultant. Public Interest Strategy & Communications was a Toronto-based consulting firm that specialized in community engagement, research, and policy development. The study argued that this involvement of outside players would prevent bias and ensure transparency of the process. The consultation process, beginning in 2002, consisted of several components including outreach and public meetings. The initial consultations helped inform the *Regent Park Revitalization Study*.[20]

According to the *Community Engagement Team Report* prior to the first consultations, the consultants conducted an environmental scan of the community.[21] This consisted of research about the neighborhood with agencies and community leaders. They identified key stakeholders and informants to help refine the framework. Based on the environmental scan, the public engagement team concluded that while residents saw living in Regent Park in a positive light, they felt it should be redeveloped. Other themes of the environmental scan included maintenance issues, a perception that living in Regent Park imposed stigma on residents, and an emphasis on safety. The public engagement team's report also documented that community members expressed a desire for a holistic approach that included more than residential buildings. Public Interest Strategy & Communications trained residents to act as facilitators called community animators. Twenty-eight community animators were hired to engage with residents during the process. This approach was identified by the Public Interest team as the "best method of reaching out to residents."[22] Public Interest claimed that the consultation process would be "entirely rooted in the community."[23] Because of time constraints, Public Interest selected animators during the environmental scan.[24] One of the main goals of the environmental scan was to identify potential community animators who were representative of the ethnocultural demographics of the community. The Engagement Report suggests that the use of animators "signif[ies] that the process was more than outreach. We wanted to convey that this process was about active engagement with the community, and the term 'animator' is a community development term that signifies 'bringing life' to a process."[25] Under this framing, the use of animators neatly aligns animation with revitalization as a process in which a community is "brought back to life." Animators were divided into animation teams that developed distinct models to consult with their respective communities and networks. Animators were each assigned a contact group and met three times with their groups to facilitate conversations about the neighborhood and potential for revitalization. The information from the groups was then shared with planners. Over the course of three months, the teams consulted 2,000 residents.[26]

The engagement team, led by Public Interest, identified three specific goals of the engagement process: ensure the community had a distinct voice in the planning process; strengthen existing and emerging community infrastructure through consultation; and assist TCHC staff in building new and effective long-term relationships with residents.[27] They asserted that meeting these goals would require "an entirely new approach," different from those employed in other contexts projects because Regent Park is a public housing project.[28]

Each phase of the process consisted of consultations with various communities within Regent Park. Many of the consultations were organized around cultural affiliation and conducted in different languages.[29] Over time the outreach program expanded to thirteen different subcommunities in Regent Park. However, some groups still felt excluded from this process—particularly the French-speaking Congolese community since meetings took place in English but not French.[30] Indigenous residents in Regent Park voiced similar concerns around their feelings of exclusion. The report described the team's ability "to defend their methodology and conclusion" and explained that "the willingness to open up the process to changes in structure involved a modest increase in workload and cost but ensured that the process retained its commitment to openness and inclusion, and was an important test in earning the trust of local residents."[31] Such reflections illustrate the tension between how some residents experienced the consultations and how planners and the engagement team understood the success of the consultations.

The *Community Engagement Team Report* consistently highlighted the difficult nature of hosting consultations in Regent Park.[32] It noted that the team recognized that "engaging residents would not be easy. Regent Park residents are a deeply impoverished multi-lingual population with a history of disappointments that has resulted in a predominant mood of mistrust and disengagement."[33] Indeed, new housing, services, and facilities had been promised to residents frequently in the past. The report described the community as potentially "cynical," saying that the engagement team would need to find a model "that informed effectively, rebuilt trust, promoted involvement and got past the cynicism" or engagement would be "nearly impossible."[34] However, the report noted triumphantly that by the end of the process, "residents dropped much of their previous cynicism and delivered a flood of data."[35]

The Regent Park revitalization framework distinguished itself from other planning frameworks at the time due to its extensive community consultations and engagement processes. The City of Toronto and TCHC adopted the consultation model to engage with other communities: "The approach used in Regent Park provides a roadmap for creating a consultation model that is truly integrated into the community and reflects not only the many faces of the population, but their cultures, processes, ideas and priorities."[36]

The Regent Park consultation process was used as a template for the Lawrence Heights Revitalization, with some key distinctions in Lawrence Heights, including the centrality of a social development plan, a *Heritage Interpretation Plan*, and the role of the Toronto District School Board. The City of Toronto listed twenty-eight consultations between 2008 and 2010; in addition to participating in these, TCHC recorded another twenty-two consultations marking the many engagement opportunities.[37] Engagement efforts in Lawrence Heights included community meetings, forums, and also the employment of community animators. One planning document highlighted that "over the past two years, there has been an extensive community consultation process that has coordinated efforts between the City, TCH and TDSB to inform the overall plan for this area."[38] A staff report for the City of

Toronto Affordable Housing Committee described collaborating with local residents as a "key component" of the revitalization process, saying it would "identify key community issues and . . . build community capacity and leadership skills in order to participate in the revitalization initiative."[39]

With the oversight of the planning committee, during the introductory stage of the consultations residents developed key definitions related to social development and revitalization, including definitions for economic development and social inclusion. The next step was to compile a document called "What We Heard," which documented residents' feedback. In November 2010, the city held an official working meeting, where residents had to preregister to attend, to begin to discuss some of the planning themes.

In Lawrence Heights, architects characterized the planning and consultation process as initiated "through an intensive period of community development, building leadership, engagement of tenants regarding revitalization [in which] TCH has supported tenants' involvement with their future. With many community forums, workshops and discussion groups, residents have talked to staff and consultants about their fears and hopes for the future."[40] The value of extensive consultation is echoed throughout the planning documents and media coverage of the revitalization. Many of the engagement activities involved youth outreach to ensure that youth voices were part of the planning process, including talent nights and activities such as photo voice and mural painting.[41] One key area was the publishing of the *Social Development Plan* in 2012. Written after consultation with residents, local organizations, and planners, the *Social Development Plan* outlined the vision for the revitalization: "We see the revitalization of Lawrence Heights as an opportunity to redefine our community and shape our future for our children, our families, and our connections with the rest of Toronto. In our vision, we see Lawrence Heights as a proud community built for the betterment of the environment and our residents. This diverse community will be enhanced through better facilities and services geared to help all members of the community succeed. Support will be needed from government agencies, residents' groups, community services, and other agencies to help empower the neighborhood during and after revitalization."[42] During the *Social Development Plan* consultation process, residents expressed a desire to preserve the history of Lawrence Heights, leading to the development of an impressive and thorough *Heritage Interpretation Plan* for Lawrence Heights. The *Heritage Plan* was created by outside consultants based on input from residents to ensure that the history and identity of the neighborhood would not be lost as a result of revitalization.

What is particularly unique about the consultation process in Lawrence Heights was tenant involvement in the selection of a developer. This was the first time that public housing tenants in Toronto were able to participate in the selection process of a developer for a revitalization project. Tenants selected one community animator to participate on the RFP selection committee and also developed a Tenant Advisory Committee that would review and rank application proposals.[43] Ultimately, in 2013, Context Development was selected as the developer and Metropia was selected as the builder in a joint venture.

Planners and some residents credited consultation and outreach for a shift in attitudes in Lawrence Heights—they described an initial reluctance and resistance from residents, but over time they suggested they were able to gain buy-in for the project. One community animator described the importance of keeping residents informed and up-to-date with information and resources. Aliyyah, the animator from Neptune who was introduced in chapter 3, summed up the animation and engagement process in general terms: "When this process began to unroll or unfold in the community, what became most important was to really inform residents about what is going on, get feedback about things that they consider priorities for their lives, and if this is really going to happen in Lawrence Heights, what are some of the things that they would like to see happen."[44] Community animators offered different reasons for wanting to get involved. One did it for money, and another who had recently moved to the community saw it as a way to get involved and meet other residents, while yet another thought animation was a way to effect change or be involved with community planning. In sum, the community engagement in Lawrence Heights involved a long-term and multifaceted process in efforts to solicit resident input.

While Lawrence Heights and Regent Park had different consultation processes, both communities outlined key community planning principles that would shape revitalization.[45] Both processes included meetings early in the planning process where residents outlined their priorities. Despite outreach and identifying core priorities, the community engagement and consultation process in Regent Park and Lawrence Heights was a point of contention for residents and planners.

Procedural Participation

Consultations in urban planning processes are a microcosm of democratic engagement where one can exercise the freedom to be engaged as a citizen.

References in interviews and planning documents describe the many consultations that were held in Regent Park and Lawrence Heights that proved planners and TCHC officials had crafted and facilitated a democratic process. Marina, a TCHC employee who worked closely with residents in Lawrence Heights, emphasized the importance of creating opportunities for what she labeled "meaningful participation" in the community engagement process. She said that she really "respect[ed]" that TCHC:

> allow[ed] us to go into communities and say, okay, our job is to work with our communities and find out and give them the opportunity to participate to, envisioning what could be here. But, to mean that. Right. So, to allow people to have meaningful participation. That it's going to make a difference. . . . You invite people to participate and to be a part of a decision-making process. And when they see that that actually happens, that is very empowering. It was empowering for me and I worked in the political process for a while. This is really very, um, meaningful. So, it is good that I can say to people let's hear your point of view on things. And know that okay, if I go back and say, people want this, it's really important to them, it is listened to. And I respect the organization for allowing that space to happen. For that dialogue, right. It is great.[46]

Marina described participation in the engagement process as "empowering" for residents and emphasized the role of the consultations to ensure dialogue. She echoed TCHC's claim that it was allowing residents to participate in democratic processes and the planning of their communities. She implied that giving residents the opportunity to participate produced empowerment. In Marina's view, participation created empowerment and was made meaningful by granting authority to residents to offer their perspective about revitalization. Her reflection "and when they see that that actually happens" references participation in the engagement process but does not denote the impact of participation on decision-making and the revitalization plans. She also suggests that her position is to transmit information from residents to TCHC ("If I go back and say, people want this . . . it is listened to"), but it does not necessitate the implementation of residents' ideas or direct decision-making powers. In the engagement process, she considered the act and performance of participation to be meaningful. Marina's reflections echo Robert Chambers's understanding of participation *as* empowerment. However, as critical development studies scholar Ilan Kapoor argues, there is a danger of equating participation with empowerment—instead, "participation as power" is often the outcome in which participation can reproduce uneven power dynamics instead of reducing or eradicating them.[47] Additionally, anti-racist feminist structural critiques highlight how communities don't need to be empowered—they already have power. Instead, their ideas, concerns, and plans might need amplification.

As a starting point to explore procedural participation, one community worker pointed out the obvious omission from the engagement process: planners never asked residents if they wanted revitalization—a claim that several community animators and residents confirmed.[48] Some residents felt the city was imposing the revitalization upon them. When I asked Tamia, an animator in Lawrence Heights, if residents were asked if they wanted revitalization, she said:

> No. That is a question that was never asked. A lot of people would be opposed. Revitalization or no revitalization? A lot of people would be opposed. A lot of people would oppose that in the sense that like, everything is going to change. People say "yes," they want revitalization. We weren't asked [if we wanted revitalization]. [At least,] I don't remember it being asked. It was already going to happen either way. So let's just see what they like in their community and what they don't like. You know? But the actual question was not asked as if we had a choice. It was already in the works. They already planned that. [Lawrence Heights is] prime land. Gentrification and whatever. . . . They already have it planned out before they come in. So, it is not like we have a definite choice to move and unmove and stuff. It was already in the works and then you come in and do your community engagement piece to rally people in.[49]

Greg, the leader of a Regent Park tenant organization, agreed: "So the consultations were more about things like the right of return and how long people would be out and who would be responsible for the moving expenses" as opposed to asking if residents wanted revitalization or wanted the mixed-income model.[50]

However, in Regent Park, community leaders involved in the revitalization referenced community efforts led by the Regent Park Resident Council (later to be called the Regent Park Neighborhood Initiative) to advocate for redevelopment in the late 1980s to redevelop the neighborhood.[51] The *Regent Park Social Development Plan* provides a one-page overview of the history of revitalization, which centers resident organizing efforts.[52] Many residents described demands made to TCHC and the City of Toronto to address the deteriorating housing stock. Several resident groups and community organizations in Regent Park were central in urging the city to redevelop the dilapidated housing stock (including the Christian Resource Center, the Regent Park Northwest Steering Committee, and the Regent Park Residents Council) in the 1990s and early 2000s. However, residents argued that while organizations did push for redevelopment and improvement of the housing stock, their push did not necessarily include the mixed-income model. Further, residents and outside critics expressed frustration when they learned that with revitalization, 266 affordable housing units would be moved outside of Regent Park (planners referred to this as "expanding the footprint" of Regent Park).

While Lawrence Heights residents did not seem to recall comparable efforts in the neighborhood, one resident told me that her neighbor would talk about community initiatives in the 1980s urging the city to address the poor quality of the buildings. In Lawrence Heights some planners reported the difficulty of getting residents to participate in consultations or buy-in to the process because of the perceived imposed nature of revitalization. In Lawrence Heights, Nick, an urban planner who worked on the revitalization, argued, "There was not a history of community activism advocating for redevelopment. It was an idea that was being brought to that community."[53] Nick argued that a lack of history of community activism advocating for redevelopment depressed participation. In contrast to Nick's explanation, residents told me that they mistrusted TCHC because of its poor performance with respect to maintenance issues that impacted their perception of the revitalization process. Engagement about the question of revitalization and the model of revitalization that requires mixed-income redevelopment is a glaring absence in the revitalization process. As Tamia asserted, revitalization "was already going to happen." This absence is just one of many communication issues in the consultation process.

When asking residents about the engagement process, residents often commented on communication among the city, TCHC, and residents. Residents described how information was not communicated nor was there effective outreach, and some argued that when residents did attend they were not listened to. Aliyyah reflected on some of the challenges with communication: "And [for the planners] that becomes difficult if [they] haven't spoken and really communicated with everybody or as many people as possible and then I think just in general with Regent Park, like, I can appreciate the consultation process. I really can. Because, yes [they] are getting feedback [from the consultation process], but [they] have to inform [residents at the same time] as [they are] collecting information because [they] can't get really accurate or relevant information from [residents] if [they] are not giving them some accurate and relevant information that they need as well."[54] In this passage, Aliyyah argues that a lack of overall communication was a problem in the consultation process that led to residents not being able to engage in meaningful participation that would have an impact on the outcome of revitalization. Instead of referencing the lack of consultation or the claim that residents were not consulted, she argues that regardless of the level of consultation, residents were not informed about the details of revitalization and therefore could not be expected to meaningfully participate.

Planners acknowledged the challenges with communication that arose in the consultation process and were not naive about the many critiques. Diana, the planner whose remarks open this chapter, attempted to explain residents' dissatisfaction:

> No one is ever going to be happy with change and that is basically the bottom line. It takes a lot of time for people to get behind the idea and there is still going to be [pause], you are never going to do anything right. Personally, this is my job armor: "This is never going to be right, and this is never going to be perfect." I mean that is really the only way. I often have meetings where people are unhappy or frustrated with what is going on and that is okay. It is their home; it is their right. Ideally, constantly that will change. It is all misinformation. So that is my other mechanism, to try to find as many different ways to get the right information out. Because people feel, "Oh, my neighbor is being pushed out."[55]

Diana described her struggles with listening to unhappy residents and appropriately communicating the necessary information to residents. She acknowledged the challenge with resident "buy-in" by saying that "it takes a lot of time for people to get behind an idea." In her view, residents' dissatisfaction was merely part of the process, and she hoped that eventually their frustration would shift. At the same time, she acknowledged concerns about displacement but felt that displacement was a myth, and she made a strong effort to inform residents that it was not true.

However, residents I interviewed frequently told me their neighbors were unaware of meetings or were misinformed about activities related to the revitalization. Although residents described written memos and updates distributed throughout the community, they also suggested that Regent Park was an oral community so people were less likely to follow updates online or through the mail. An active community leader in Lawrence Heights described a lack of information and communication. He said that even though he worked in the community center and was the head of a leading youth organization in the neighborhood, he was unaware of the dates and times of meetings and did not know anyone who was involved or attended. When I spoke with him, there were basic pieces of information about the revitalization process that were unclear to him, including the timeline and overall revitalization framework (mixed-use and mixed-income). Similarly, Tamia described the difficulties of communicating necessary information to the community:

> I guess, at times it was easy for me because I am a people person, but at times it was challenging in the sense that, like, we are trying, like [pause], there are how many residents in Lawrence Heights? But I don't really feel like we get to the masses. Like, it is the same people over and over again. What about the hidden youth? Like, youth that don't really come out. I will talk to them when they come out, but you never get these youth [pause], I don't feel that we reach, like, who needs to be reached. It is the people that [are] in the know [who attend meetings]. But I guess like people see that phase one is going to affect them and they will run out to a meeting and make some noise and stuff like that, but again, it is just the people that [are] in the know. The regular people you will see but there [are] a lot of people who still don't know.[56]

Tamia critiqued the engagement processes' ability to reach residents and the "hidden" populations that were missed. For Tamia, it was only residents who were "in the know" who participated. This reflects the performative nature of participation—a process exists, forums are scheduled, people are invited, but it does not necessarily facilitate meaningful engagement where there is a broad representation of residents or where residents are involved in decision-making and have an impact on the outcomes in a way that they envision to be meaningful.

Andrea, the executive director of a community service organization in Regent Park, described a shift in the effectiveness of the consultations. TCHC recruited her to help support the consultation efforts in Regent Park. She described the early stages as "effective": "My experience with TCH was that TCH and the city were, in my view, really effective in making sure that they consulted, in doing the best they could at that time when they were still in the approval process. That they engaged with the agencies and the community residents as best as they could." However, she felt that the consultation process changed over time: "We have had situations where things don't get communicated. TCH hasn't done thinking about who is going to come to those meetings and it's like they don't understand the community. We have been in situations where we find out about decisions that have been made that we find out about it afterwards." Andrea's frustration with finding out about decisions after they were made include her reference to the Regent Park Centre of Learning discussed in chapter 2. She went on to argue, "However, now that [the plan] has been approved and it has been rolled out, things changed, terribly. Like, a lot. And I understand that things change, because opportunities come up that were not seen. And all of it is about getting money to set up the resources. So, there is not an inclusive approach to that kind of process."[57] Andrea gave specific examples of breakdowns of communication in the process. She described meetings where residents were not adequately informed, there was not enough space, and there were no translators. This last item was particularly galling; meetings in Regent Park always had translation, an obvious requirement given the linguistic range of residents. This would seem like a clear violation of the value of diversity and promotion of diversity that were explored in chapter 2. Theoretical references to diversity and inclusion via participation did not transfer into practice. Rather than implementing inclusive practices, procedural participation did not facilitate spaces where impactful and transformative participation could occur.

Residents' views on the lack of substantive democratic engagement reflect a neoliberal incarnation of formalized or thin democracy. Merhawit is a doctor from East Africa who moved to Canada with her husband and children. She was active in the Lawrence Heights community and regularly spoke about her work in the community garden. Merhawit described her frustration about the reporting of a survey she helped to construct and distribute to 500 residents in Lawrence Heights. When the city reported the findings, she felt discouraged and disheartened by the results. She reported that many of the findings were not included in the report and that the data were misrepresented. Benjamin, who lived in the middle-upper-income Lawrence Manor neighborhood adjacent to Lawrence Heights that was peppered with signs that read "Save Our Streets" in opposition to the revitalization, expressed frustration and anger about the consultation process. Benjamin was active in local politics and he was unforgiving in his scathing critique of the revitalization. While he acknowledged that there were different consultation events, he characterized the procedural nature of the process by describing it as "flawed," "top down," and "authoritarian":

There were consultations where one person spoke and held the podium and people came up with ideas but were not allowed to interact with one another or another where there were small working tables where people didn't get to interact and develop ideas at length. So, the structure of that planning process was flawed. It was top down. It was authoritarian. The minutes were not set by the community. The minutes were set by planning staff and, quite frankly, there was an abuse of process. There were two meetings held back to back on consecutive evenings and they resulted in increasing divisiveness between owners and tenants. At the meeting which would be held for people who would most easily be described as independent homeowners, they were told that the laneways between Lawrence Heights and the communities to the east and west would not be opened, that they would be enhanced in terms of bicycle paths but that they would never be opened. The very next night the audience that was primarily comprised of tenants, they heard a different message. A block is being put on those laneways so that at a future time they could be made open. Another problem is that you need to understand is that many of the residents living in Lawrence Heights are a) not familiar with English and b) have two or three jobs, so the number of residents that are attending those meetings, notwithstanding that there were free food and beverages, notwithstanding the fact that there was day care, was relatively small. A very, very, very small percentage.[58]

The issue Benjamin referenced with the laneways was a major point of contention between TCHC residents in Lawrence Heights and homeowners in Lawrence Manor. Lawrence Heights residents wanted to be connected with the surrounding neighborhoods through these laneways; Lawrence Manor residents did not want them to be connected because of the increase of density and traffic it would bring to Lawrence Manor.

Lawrence Manor is located directly east of Lawrence Heights. A fence separates the two communities. Residents of Lawrence Manor organized a "Save Our Streets" campaign to stop the revitalization. They argued, among other things, that the area could not support the planned increase in density. However, Aliyyah described these tensions as reflecting prejudice:

Just based on the general dynamics of community itself: you have Lawrence Manor residents who have been staunchly against this happening or this process, as well. You know a lot of that comes down to arguments around density. But some of that is a lack of understanding because the revit[alization] means that there is going to be an increase in population in the area. It also means that their assumptions . . . I noticed a lot of times [people say] "you guys are gonna bring twenty thousand welfare people to the community." So, there is a little bit of miscommunication or lack of understanding as well. And you know there's a little bit of a sense of us and them with this conversation . . . you know . . . so we [meaning Lawrence Manor residents] don't want "them" here. We don't want them in our schools. We don't want that on our streets..[59]

Aliyyah described the underlying race and class stereotypes that paint Lawrence Heights residents as undesirable neighbors. Aliyyah was skeptical of the participation of residents of Lawrence Manor who she argued discriminated against Lawrence Heights residents and stigmatized them for being low-income. Several Lawrence Heights residents generally felt that the surrounding communities opposed the revitalization because of racism, and they made their feelings known in the deputations at a June 22, 2010, North York Council meeting I attended and in its aftermath. Benjamin, however, recounted that the city contributed to the conflict between the two neighborhoods by presenting different information to each group during consultations.

Eva, a Regent Park resident, echoed claims saying that residents were not "heard." Of the consultations, Eva recalled: "You know what. They asked so many things. 'What would you like?' 'What would you want?' 'And what didn't you like?' A lot of people didn't show up. Like I said, people are fed up of going to meetings and not being heard—being ignored. So, a lot of people didn't bother going. They didn't bother going. . . . I went to all of [the meetings]. But . . . the promise has not been kept so people don't bother."[60] Both Merhawit and Eva highlight that residents' felt their participation was not meaningful or that in general, residents' input was not heard or ignored, yet both remained actively engaged. Tamia explained this as well:

I see a lot of information. Because I have been out there from the first stage, like drafting the original surveys. Like "what do you like about Lawrence Heights?" We talked about the greenery, the open space and stuff like that and people say . . . I could go on and on and on . . . but when you see the draft plans and stuff . . . you can't really meet everybody's needs. *But the stuff that people want is not really taken into consideration* [emphasis added]. . . . I don't see how we had input in the final plan. At the end of the day, I just think it was just the big wigs; they hear what we have to say but they have something up their sleeve. I don't feel that those meetings were effective.[61]

Merhawit's, Eva's, and Tamia's reflections on the process mark how there were multiple opportunities to participate and give input, but that residents' ideas and requests were in fact not represented in consultation summaries or in the final plans. While residents participated in different forums or filled out surveys, the engagement opportunities were a stage for the performance of a participatory process that did not necessitate participation that would in fact inform the revitalization process.

Similarly, Aliyyah commented on the engagement process but framed her understanding around the "powerlessness" of low-income residents:

> To be very honest, anything in a society where you are that powerless—one, there is always a certain dose of a realistic fear around, what does this mean for me? How much ability do I have to advocate for myself when things are being changed or when things are changing? And you know, for the majority of the people, they know that this change is happening above their heads regardless if they go and say we want this or we don't want this. To a very large degree it is going to happen. Right? So, you get a sense that you don't have much power in this kind of larger society.[62]

Aliyyah felt that the consultations did not put change in residents' reach; it remained "above their heads." Despite voicing their hopes and aspirations ("if they go and say we want this or we don't want this"), residents in Lawrence Heights were marginalized in a process that claims to be founded on principles of inclusion and as a microcosm of Canadian democracy. Aliyyah went on to explain:

> There is a very healthy or real sense of that at the end of the day, I can demand as much as I want, but the decision does not lie in my hands and I think that is really [pause], the things that are happening above our heads is those decisions don't happen or don't rest in our hands. And I mean it's just generally in a society where things [pause], it's very much a power dynamic. So, there are certain bodies in the community that can say this is what we want, and they do have a lot more buying power than others. . . . So, you realize that you can do so much . . . but there is so much that can be done without you.[63]

Aliyyah reiterated that residents had limited power to make decisions. She expected the city and the residents of wealthier neighborhoods to have more control. As she noted, residents could make demands and collectively organize, but the power dynamic makes it difficult to have a material impact. As residents of a low-income housing project—the very characterization that makes the neighborhood in need of revitalization—she and her neighbors were invited to participate, but the process limited their ability to have an impact.

While Aliyyah suggested that wealthier communities had a greater voice, Benjamin, who lived to Lawrence Manor, also felt unheard: "But there is anger out there; there is bitterness out there that we were not consulted . . . that the city is not consultative and were looking for ways to express that they were upset and that dissatisfaction. And there were people that were very, very upset and remain so."[64] Benjamin agreed that the planners had not listened to resident feedback: "We had a number of ideas. Would they all have worked? Maybe. Maybe not. But they were not listened to."[65] Benjamin's characterization of the anger of residents due to the city's lack of consultation corresponds to a general sentiment of dissatisfaction among residents whom I interviewed.

Alongside resident critiques about communication and the misrepresentation or underrepresentation of resident feedback were questions about the transparency of the process. Diana, who facilitated the consultations in Lawrence Heights, acknowledged:

> I think we are often not very good communicators. And we often wonder why we don't take the time to say um, "I don't know. I'm not sure—let me get back to you." Or "we don't have an answer" . . . because we are under a lot of pressure to be really responsive to the community and then we make promises and we can't keep them . . . and then we should say, "Let's just be honest. We can't do this; we tried our best; these are the reasons. We are doing this to mitigate and compensate, but we still have to move forward." We are not that good at that kind of stuff always. I think if we were better communicators, um, at just being—and also having faith to reason with the process, then I think we would save ourselves a lot of headaches. But that goes for everything in general and stuff. So, we are trying to come up with solutions when all we have to do is say sorry.[66]

While Diana acknowledged that communication was often not particularly effective, residents' sentiments imply that planners were right to feel that residents would not accept apologies for the failure to be responsive. Benjamin, for example, stated:

> I was at one of the first meetings where they were talking about principles. Three different people stood up and said, "Preservation is a principle." The next meeting, [residents] said, "What about that preservation? It is still not in your literature," [and they said], "Oh, no, no, no. It is here. We are just gathering it together." You will not find that word [preservation] anywhere in the report. They were not listening. Now maybe that makes for expeditious planning when you have a very strong willed, dominant councilor. But it does not make for community planning. And the notion that there was any kind of legitimate planning, I reject wholly.[67]

Benjamin's comments imply that he would not excuse planners' ignoring input during consultations. He identified a breakdown in communication and suggested this made the planning process and consultations illegitimate. Benjamin's account is an example of procedural participation. If communication is seen as a barrier to effective consultation on behalf of residents and planners, yet the consultations are continuously described as successful, then it does not much matter what or how ideas are communicated and if they make a difference.

Chandra, a former Regent Park resident and community worker reported,

> We have had a history in the community where the people who were already in support of something, from the powers that be, were called to the meeting and then you see later that the community was consulted and dadadada, but you know that there were twenty people who tend to be . . . or they pick people who are already working in that direction or the same people over and over and over again, and you miss completely huge groups of populations that weren't even in the meeting and talking about things around young people and the youth with no youth there, you know and looking at the way we do things. You know, are meetings really accessible? And the challenge of having limited resources and high needs. Multi and complex, layers upon layers upon layers of vulnerable, marginalized folks.[68]

Chandra expressed a need to go beyond the required procedures of scheduling a meeting in order to authentically engage with a range of residents and generate dialogue between residents and planners. She pointed to the procedural nature of the process by suggesting that the consultations recruited people who were already in support of certain ideas or that the same groups of residents attended the consultations and therefore did not necessarily represent the different voices in the community. Her perspective that "people who were already in support of something . . . they pick people who are already working in that direction," or "the same people over and over again" alongside reports that "the community was consulted" signals the procedural nature of the process. While there were consultations, Chandra highlighted the limitations of the consultations. Overall, there were concerns about the circulation of information and the actual consultation meetings; some thought this led to low turnout or limited responses from the community. TCHC and the city claimed that they employed many different formats to communicate information to residents, but some residents felt it had been inadequate or was not transparent.[69]

Contesting Community Consultation

In my second conversation with Merhawit, the active Lawrence Heights community member who participated in multiple aspects of the engagement process and supported revitalization, she explained to me that the consultation process entailed residents sitting in rooms with planners at the front "instructing" them.[70] Merhawit described the power dynamic in the consultation process: "It is just like someone ordering [you around] and [you] taking the order kind of thing. And residents felt that [planners] are going to do whatever they are going to do. Why would we get involved? . . . But, that is not true. People do have voices and people do have power and, on that line, I think that the residents have realized that they could make an impact on whatever is going to happen in the community. *Even if nothing is done, it is good to know your rights and push for your rights*" [emphasis added].[71] Merhawit insisted that it was important to voice concerns and ideas regardless of whether their input would be used in the plans. Here, residents' sense of power did not come from implementation; instead, residents felt powerful and motivated by their ability to self-mobilize and participate in the planning process. While at one point she described planners giving orders to residents during consultations, Merhawit also compared the meeting to a classroom setting where she and other residents were students and planners were teachers—residents were being talked "at" and not engaged in dialogue. However, she was passionate about having rights and having a voice in the process. She consistently emphasized the importance of the community's agency and the fact that neighbors were coming together to organize around issues that affect their everyday lives. Her reflection that "it is good to know your rights and push for your rights" does not focus on a lack of decision-making power for residents in the revitalization process but instead highlights how the process produces an opportunity for residents to become aware of what is happening in their neighborhood and to collectively fight for what they want beyond revitalization. She acknowledged the cynicism of some residents who asked, "Why would we get involved?" because planners were "going to do whatever they were going to do." Her sharp reply, "That is not true," followed by an articulation of the power of resident voice and potential for impact, is an articulation of contested consultation. She characterized the impact of participation thus:

> But people at the beginning thought, why do you go to those meetings? No change is going to happen. But they do realize now if possible, they do want to participate. Um, people have lots of kids, young kids and it is not easy to . . . the number of meetings there were . . . it was too much. I had to stretch myself to do it because I thought there was the need, but now people are definitely empowered. Definitely. They voiced [how] they have upgraded themselves. In the past they had the "what can I do?" kind of attitude. People are upgrading themselves in different ways. And I am happy to see that.[72]

Merhawit explained that even though it was difficult for her to make time in her busy schedule to participate, she was still compelled to do so because she saw a need. Merhawit suggested that "residents are upgrading themselves" by participating, even though she had acknowledged that "no change is going to happen" and that residents had little hope of influencing the plan—especially in light of her critique that the survey findings were not accurately represented. By "upgrading," Merhawit captures how residents created their own sense of power that came from amplifying their voices. Merhawit became involved in the process as a way to "better" herself and her community. Merhawit's insights shed light on residents' broader vision of transformation that was not necessarily about revitalization. Similarly, Merhawit described the gardens and parks of Lawrence Heights as communal spaces where residents could come together and talk about issues that affect the community—describing that these were also spaces where residents discussed revitalization and transformation outside of the formal consultation process.

When I asked Tamia, a Lawrence Heights resident and animator, if she felt like she made a difference in the process, she laughed and said:

That is a good question. Yes and no. Yes, in the sense that I love the whole community animation process because it is community: residents talking with other community residents. You know, so put a personal spin on it. But at the same time . . . at times I get all of this information and this training but at times I just feel like a scapegoat . . . [Like] I am being used. I am on the front line. . . . but I feel like as a community animator residents trust me because I am putting a personal spin on it because it affects me and it affects them and I am relaying the information from what I am given, but sometimes I feel I am just being used for that purpose.[73]

Tamia expressed concerns that the planners were using her to sell the revitalization or give the appearance of receiving residents' feedback ("I am being used"). As an animator, someone who worked as both a bridge to the planners and a representative of them to residents in Lawrence Heights, Tamia entered the process believing she would be helping to promote participation and engagement. However, she was taken aback by residents' discomfort and skepticism about the process and the planners. She also felt that Public Interest Strategy & Communications should have had an ongoing involvement in the process. Their training had impressed her because it helped her understand how to avoid bias, but their disappearance from the process was one of the factors that made her feel that TCHC was not responsive to residents. She also noted that Public Interest had not trained animators who joined in the second year of the consultation process. Ultimately, Tamia saw the animation process as part of what she labeled a "front" by TCHC. She reported discomfort and conflicting association with the consultations. She liked the idea of working with her neighbors and informing residents of the process. However, she also felt that planners were "us[ing]" her and other animators and that TCHC was influencing the process too much.

While Tamia was in favor of the continued role of Public Interest, which she saw as an outside influence that would temper TCHC's desire to control the process, a local community newspaper published an editorial warning of Public Interest's role in the process under the headline "TCH Tenants: Watch out for Public Interest."[74] The newspaper criticized Public Interest's "bogus" consultations and accused them of "selling the idea of redevelopment to the people." The editorial also describes a push by the editor of the paper and another resident to encourage an independent tenant initiative that was not funded by TCHC.

Like Tamia, Aliyyah expressed multilayered sentiments about the consultations. Aliyyah critiqued the process, but she also argued that residents were heard. When I asked her if she thought residents were heard, she said:

> I would have to say yes, based on what we've seen so far. [Toronto Community] Housing has made a real commitment . . . and [Toronto Community] Housing more so than the city, has made a real commitment, a real, real commitment to do this work with the community. . . . So, the preferred plan and then how they were going to go about phase one, and phase two, I can see that they really have been listening to what people have been saying to them, but definitely what the animators have been saying to them. So, I can see in those kind of small or different pieces they have been really listening to what people have been saying. To balance this and essentially try to keep as many people satisfied as possible. Not necessarily happy. But satisfied for the time being, as possible. So, yes, I'd say they've committed to that as well.[75]

Aliyyah suggested that TCHC and the city made a commitment to effectively consult with residents. However, previously Aliyyah had also described the decision-making process as excluding residents.[76] There were many disjunctures both in individual residents' own thinking about the consultation process and also between residents. This does not reveal an inconsistency that would make the claims irrelevant; rather, I suggest it is a glimpse into contested consultation where residents contested the formal consultation process and made sense of the possibilities for transformation via critique and nuance, not contradiction.

Greg, a community leader in Regent Park, described the complicated nature of the engagement process and participation:

> I think if you wanted to give an opinion, that it would reach the planners and the architects and the city. There were a lot of people who didn't want to give an opinion or didn't believe that it would be heard and therefore did not give an opinion. And those people were not heard. But that is the same as if in an election you don't vote, then you don't vote. That was their choice. Some people I guess were not comfortable in those settings and they might not have been heard. But if they knew somebody that was somewhat involved and you just walk up to them and talk to them and then to a large extent you were heard, too.[77]

Greg's response begins with a very straightforward account that residents could provide input and it would be taken into consideration. However, he then described the hesitation and resistance to participate by some residents. He framed participation as a "choice" by residents and attributed this choice to a lack of feeling comfortable in the official consultation settings and acknowledged that "they might not have been heard." Some residents, in Greg's account, had strong enough conviction *not* to participate because of a belief that they would not be heard; according to Greg, some residents did not participate because they believed their ideas would not be considered or implemented in the planning process. In the end, however, Greg still maintained that if residents wanted to voice an opinion, planners were willing to listen.

Both Aliyyah and Greg offer contrasting accounts about residents' communication and whether their voices were "heard." The struggle over communication demonstrates how residents conceptualized the consultation process and had differing ideas about whether or not to participate. Residents' decisions as to whether to participate were nuanced negotiations that underscore longer histories of exclusion. A transformative aspect of consultations was not about whether information was received or if it had an impact, but because people spoke up about issues that were important to the community and their everyday lives regardless of their belief that their input was considered.

In addition to debates around communication and if residents were heard, there were concerns about transparency. For example, Chandra noted, "So even with the communication that we did have, there was always still this sense that there was always something happening that we were not part of."[78] Residents and agency staff frequently referenced a lack of transparency and open communication. Sheila, the former Regent Park resident who was displaced by the revitalization (featured in chapter 3), described planners as secretive, even deceitful: "Like you could tell that there were secretly things . . . that they didn't want to let out, like they didn't want to let it out to the press or something."[79] A lack of transparency produced and furthered residents' skepticism about the consultations. For some residents, the concern over truthful and open information called into question the legitimacy of the consultations and is another marker of community contestation, where residents named the specific power dynamics at play in the consultations and challenged dominant narratives that described an inclusive process when in fact, many residents felt invited in only to be systematically excluded.

One resident, Kaydeen, reflected on the frustration that emerged from participating, only to have important aspects of the revitalization jeopardized: "Over the years, however, as staff changed, some of the initiatives that had come out of the older community consultations, such as the Heritage and Social Development Plans, seemed to fall by the wayside, only kept alive by concerted advocacy efforts from the community. The future of the new community center, promised as part of phase two of the revitalization project, is now in question, with building stalled after the provincial government withheld funding."[80] Tenants expressed concerns about the process and the changing of staff and failed promises. Kaydeen described how administrative challenges, including changes of staff and the long planning process, contributed to the potential disappearance of initiatives that emerged in consultations. These very real administrative hurdles throughout consultation processes, along with community outreach over a long period of time, highlight how engagement and the design of consultations can lead residents to question what happened to the ideas they shared. However, Kaydeen shines a spotlight on how the resident insights referenced in the *Social Development Plan* and the *Heritage Plan* were "kept alive by concerted advocacy efforts from the community." While employees tasked with engagement and consultation may come and go, residents held long-standing historical community memory and persisted in their critiques around funding and ensuring community voices were amplified on their own terms.

Residents' skepticism produced alternate understandings of the revitalization and offered a critique of the processes of exclusion that they were experiencing. Their decision to participate or not participate was about their own visions of community, regardless of how the planners framed consultations. Even though many residents saw communication as ineffective, they still made meaning of their worlds and possibilities through formal and informal channels of participation.

Conclusion

Marina, the TCHC employee who worked closely with residents in Lawrence Heights, argued that civic engagement and decision-making were central to an "ideal" neighborhood: "An ideal neighborhood is the people . . . have good housing, that they have adequate levels of the income, they have supports that they need. And then it's a place where people are able to [access] opportunities for civic engagement, opportunities for democratic participation in their lives. They have an opportunity for decision-making on issues that affect them in their communities." Marina described consultations, like many planning documents, as a way to promote civic engagement and democratic participation, similar to Diana's reference to teaching residents to be Canadian that opened this chapter. However, the construction of consultations simultaneously operates as a national identity-making technology that limited possibilities of participation for residents. The revitalization engagement process signaled the operationalizing of democracy, even as the larger framework of revitalization speaks to constrained possibilities for participation. More concisely, consultation is a procedural requirement versus a substantive democratic practice. The consultations mobilized a particular type of participation that was dependent on generic performances of participation where the content of engagement does not much matter. Emphasis on *rituals of democracy*, like participation, can legitimize the neoliberal model of revitalization.[81] As Tamia pointed out, Lawrence Heights residents were asked about many aspects of the revitalization, but not whether they wanted revitalization or their opinion about the mixed-income model and the financial framework. Merhawit and others expressed concerns about the mixed-income model and a fear of what it would do to the fabric of their community and how new middle-income residents would treat residents who lived in RGI units.[82]

Procedural participation legitimizes the neoliberal model of revitalization. As highlighted in the opening section on procedural participation, while residents were consulted about many aspects of the process, one non-negotiable feature was the neoliberal economic model (mixed-income sustained by a public-private partnership). In summary, procedural participation *positions* engagement as an opportunity for perceived immigrant, racialized as nonwhite, and low-income subjects to practice participation (like voting in an election) promoting Canadian ideals around democracy and inclusion, but ultimately limits participation or belonging.

Residents' varying perspectives challenged procedural consultation practices through cynicism about the likely impact of engagement (e.g., voter apathy) and also critiqued the process of consultation as democratic engagement. Tamia mused, "Yes, they have the process in place, I'm not gonna lie. But at the end of the day is it reflective of what we want? I don't think so." In Tamia's view, the end product or outcome of the consultations did not reflect residents' input. Beyond this cynicism, residents also had a strong politicized response and sought to amplify residents' voices illuminating powerful micropolitics at the community level. For residents like Tamia, Sheila, Chandra, and Eva, the consultations gave them informal opportunities to critique the overall revitalization process and their exclusion from it.

In short, residents created possibilities of being that exist beyond constrained institutionalized consultation practices. Chandra articulated the multiple levels of contestation through what she called "community ownership":

> Well, residents believed that we told you stuff and now we want to see it. And if we told you all this stuff and we are not seeing it then you did not really listen, it was just an exercise. . . . There are some places where residents don't feel that though their voices were provided that they were acknowledged. I will tell you that the community did not want to lose any RGIs [rent-geared-to-income units], and as those numbers change and this progression goes on, and it looks like the end of the build-out the RGI population will only be twenty-six percent of the total. So, [she laughed] developing trust and keeping engaged and really feeling that sense of presence that you were involved in the decisions, not just the discussions and then they went off and made the decisions.[83]

Here, Chandra describes procedural participation as an exercise that had no impact on the revitalization plans. Her reference to RGI units points out that some aspects of the revitalization, including the financial framework as a whole, were pre-established and not included in the consultations. These aspects of the revitalization not raised in the consultations mirror those that dominate the hierarchy of diversity discussed in chapter 2.

Beyond Chandra's critique of the revitalization, her overall concern is that of community ownership. Consultations imply participation and residents having a voice in the revitalization and design of their communities. For Chandra, the concept of community ownership is not solely about participation but meaningful involvement that will implement change and centers residents as leading the process and as decision makers. Residents accepted that communication is not necessarily straightforward, so they find other ways to make it meaningful. For residents, this is about collaboration and promotes epistemologies that emerge from collective and transformative participation.

Conclusion

> By the 1970s, what had been long represented, according to
> dominant historical narratives of the nation, as the core Canadian
> cultural identity—Anglo-white—was in need of serious revision
> and reconstruction. Through the concept of multiculturalism,
> a new story of the Canadian nation was developed, one that
> recognized this diversity and sought to construct a unified Canadian
> identity through the harmonization or reconciliation of this ethnic
> difference—unity was to be found in diversity.
> —BRIAN, "Recognition Politics," 123.

Tesfaye, a politically engaged resident from Lawrence Heights, spoke at a North York Community Council meeting on June 22, 2010, about the surrounding "Canadian neighborhoods."[1] When I later asked Tesfaye what he meant by "Canadian," he responded, "When I say Canadian, we are all Canadians, but when you are isolated by a fence and you cannot walk to other neighborhoods, that means that you are not Canadian, you are confined and isolated and maybe some people just come from Africa and they are put here and they are still not Canadian even though by paper they have their citizenship. They cannot walk in every direction to other neighborhoods. So, they are not integrated. They are not Canadian."[2] Tesfaye spoke about the fence that separated Lawrence Heights from Lawrence Manor that was discussed in chapter 4. He critiqued the material construction of the neighborhood and how it contributed to his sense of exclusion. Because of material and structural boundaries, Lawrence Heights residents were separated from the neighboring communities and the city as a whole. For Tesfaye, being Canadian is related to being part of a broader society and not separated from other Canadians by a fence—a material spatial construction to maintain race and class disparity and segregation. By asserting that in spite of citizenship, the fence makes Lawrence Heights residents "not Canadian," he suggested that entrenched disparity attenuated claims about inclusiveness in Canada.

Tesfaye also imagined an alternative to exclusion and stigmatization. He went on to say, "If there is a healthy integration there would be participation in meetings together, children could play together. Then that is real participation. That is the Canadian way, really." Tesfaye talked about the fence and the isolation caused by the built environment *alongside* the revitalization consultation meetings. For Tesfaye, there should have been space in the revitalization planning process for residents of Lawrence Heights and other communities to come together, where children could play and adults could interact. Tesfaye's reflections signal what he viewed as a missed opportunity in the consultation process. His phrasing "if there is healthy integration" indexes his critique of the process and the lack of what he deemed "real participation." His reference to the "Canadian way," coupled with his comments about real participation and children playing together, align Canadianness with his different examples of inclusion, community, and belonging. Tesfaye's insights capture the layers of precarity and marginalization that are materially and discursively reinforced in revitalization, as well as possibilities for what he calls healthy integration and an alternative to spatial and social segregation.

In *On Being Included*, Sara Ahmed argues, "Inclusion could be read as a technology of governance: not only as a way of bringing those who have been recognized as strangers into the nation, but also of making strangers into subjects, those who in being included are also willing to consent to the terms of inclusion."[3] She goes on to write, "Being included can be a lesson in 'being not' as much as 'being in.'" In other words, inclusion as a technology does not necessitate being welcomed as part of a group or community; in fact, it can reveal the limitations of inclusion and require exclusion. Ahmed's framing of inclusion as a technology of governance pushes us to consider how inclusion is one way to signal recognition—a central aspect of multicultural governance. I draw from these conceptualizations of power and technology in the context of cities and urban governance. *Precarious Constructions* sheds light on the many tensions in residents' engagement with revitalization and contradictions in the process itself. Although some residents were critical of the process, they also affirmed ideals articulated in terms of diversity, Canadianness, and the potential opportunities made available through revitalization.

Interventions

One of the main aims of this book is to map how revitalization is central to the nation's articulation of racial logics. The framework of urban revitalization, like many projects of neoliberal multicultural integration, simultaneously presupposes the racial and class inferiority of residents and obscures the structural causes of racial and class segregation. By zooming in on two Toronto neighborhoods and examining specific constructions of urban governance via revitalization, *Precarious Constructions* highlights how neoliberal multiculturalism is tied to the unstable construction of national identity, as well as how residents question and negotiate the limitations of the bureaucratic employment of diversity, surveillance, and participation.

Another key aim of this work is to illustrate how neoliberal multiculturalism operates across time, space, and context. By mapping the shift from welfare state housing provisions that were put in place to secure and stabilize a labor force to the neoliberal retrenchment of welfare state policies and contemporary revitalization, close examination of the planning process demonstrates how purportedly progressive efforts to address housing segregation obscure and reproduce inequality. What emerges is an analysis of the material and discursive ways that inequality is reproduced: the material-built environment—including public housing neighborhoods—is intimately intertwined with discourses around diversity, surveillance, and participation. While the material and discursive, as well as diversity, surveillance, and participation, are usually treated as distinct or separate, they are interconnected in social regulation efforts such as urban revitalization. By examining how they build on one another, we can disrupt assumptions about the construction and fundamental nature of each:

Diversity: By understanding diversity as constructed and produced via modes of governance, we can disrupt the ways it is often situated as an equity term that emerges from embodiment. Instead, diversity becomes connected to both surveillance and participation. The presumed diversity of a particular neighborhood can become a justification for increased policing based on racialization and stigmatization.

Surveillance: Surveillance is often understood alongside to policing. In the case of "eyes on the street," I show how surveillance conscripts residents into participating in policing one another in the name of community building or community safety. In Regent Park and Lawrence Heights, eyes on the street is framed in relation to the diversity of the neighborhoods and their stigmatization as crime ridden and unsafe spaces despite residents' articulation of having a strong sense of community and their critique of stigmatization of their communities.

Participation: In the case of participation, community consultations script and constrain the meaning and function of diversity.

Consultations were often articulated in relation to residents' immigrant status and positioned as a tool for inclusion. However, consultations limited and regulated participation in ways that ultimately reproduced residents' exclusion via their very inclusion in consultations.

In short, while diversity, surveillance, and consultation are constructed as positive aspects of the revitalization process that can address sociospatial inequality, their contested coconstitution as tools in the revitalization process is central to social regulation via neoliberal multiculturalism. They are constructed and mobilized to legitimize the revitalization process both discursively and materially—in the planning documents as well as in the built environment and the urban landscape. In sum, *Precarious Constructions* shows how this coconstitution of diversity, surveillance, and participation becomes integral to the reproduction of societal power relations and hierarchies through discursive and material planning processes.

While there is established scholarly engagement with the various topics this book takes up, including revitalization, gentrification, diversity, multiculturalism, neoliberalism, surveillance, and consultations, *Precarious Constructions* examines the deceptive coarticulation of these social processes and dynamics. By developing the frame of precarious constructions, I aim to denaturalize how these currents inform the construction of housing, the construction of subjectivity, the construction of belonging, and the construction of inequality. Although these concepts are often taken for granted or analyzed as stable or neutral, I analyze how the mobilization alongside the cachet of multiculturalism facilitates the deceptive reproduction of inequality under the auspices of inclusion.

I consider the impact of gentrification on the contemporary urban landscape as a starting place to examine how entangled projects of multiculturalism and neoliberalism shape belonging and inclusion on the one hand, and inequality and exclusion on the other. Revitalization in Lawrence Heights and Regent Park cannot live up to its promises of equity and addressing longstanding racial and class segregation. This line of inquiry points to broader questions about the limits of efforts around "diversity, equity, and inclusion" that dominate institutional discussions purportedly aiming to address longstanding structural inequalities. *Precarious Constructions* reveals that such progressive efforts mask how that diversity can stand in for disparity and inequality, calls for safety require criminalization, and consultation legitimizes the process but limits engagement and participation. Although this investigation focuses on two Toronto neighborhoods, the ubiquity of "diversity talk," the criminalization of populations racialized as nonwhite, and generic consultation and engagement processes suggest broader implications for understanding how inequality is materially and discursively reproduced and entrenched under the guise of neoliberal multiculturalism.

Placemaker and city-builder Jay Pitter's reflections on Regent Park push us to consider challenges with revitalization. She writes,

> Ensuring there were a variety of affordable rental units, market townhomes and condominiums, recreational and cultural facilities, and businesses was a good start. Few would argue with the ideal of a diversity of residents raising families, learning, enjoying green space and working alongside each other. But many outsiders, including planners and community development advocates, might overlook the complexity of the residual issues stemming from the community's legacy of poor design and systemic marginalization, and its ongoing challenges with crime and safety. What's more, they may not understand the sense of loss felt by long-time residents, and the lingering class tensions that surface when affluent condo buyers move into a space that most of the city once avoided.[4]

Pitter's sharp insights highlight the need to situate any analysis of revitalization in a broader historical and spatial context. The sociospatial history and segregation of neighborhoods should be foundational to addressing urban inequality. *Precarious Constructions* engages with the relationship between the construction of the built environment and urban planning to consider how such processes organize our social worlds and contribute to the reproduction of structural inequality and precarity.

Housing Justice

Housing is an often taken-for-granted aspect of society—especially by those who have access to safe and secure housing options via wealth or upward mobility. This book examines how public housing is reorganized in relation to urban governance discourses such as diversity, surveillance, and consultations and asserts that the construction of housing options and access to affordable housing are social justice issues that deserves continued analysis.

Interventions into how we approach and understand housing have the potential to contribute to housing justice and broader political struggles. Houselessness, long housing waitlists, inadequate housing, affordable housing options, and maintenance backlogs in public housing are structural problems that require structural solutions. They are also issues that may appear to signal a lack of political will and priorities that are in many cases beyond the scope of urban planning. However, attributing such failures to political representation ignores the necessary critiques of liberal rights–based discourse and the many shortcomings of liberal democracy that in fact fundamentally require vulnerability and precarity.

While governments often stumble and become entangled in bureaucracy and ideological debates, communities have long presented and created plans to address housing needs. Below is a list of interconnected interventions that present sketches of preliminary options to address the state's inability to meet one of the most basic human needs. Notably, many of these ideas are proven community-based solutions that have emerged from community organizing by people racialized as nonwhite, poor and low-income, feminist, and/or queer communities. These intertwined structural interventions move beyond the push for "housing as a human right" to call into question the limitations of liberal rights–based frameworks and instead promote structural and sustainable solutions despite the limitations of neoliberal democracy. Further, these interventions address the problems and inequality that emerge when housing is constructed as a commodity.[5]

1. *A national housing guarantee*

   A national housing guarantee would ensure equitable housing options for all people. All residents would be provided with safe and affordable housing options that are guaranteed by federal policies and supported with federal, provincial, and local funding.

2. *Guaranteed basic income*

   A national guaranteed basic income would address income disparity and give people the opportunity to permanently afford safe housing. While Ontario launched a Basic Income Pilot Project in 2017 under the liberal government of Premier Kathleen Wynne, it was canceled in July 2020 under Premier Doug Ford. However, the findings of the project revealed that the recipients were still motivated to find employment and work (despite critics' warnings that if given a basic income they would not continue or seek employment—a similar argument that underpins ideas around the value of mixed-income housing and influencing behaviors) and enjoyed better overall health and well-being than prior to their participation in the project.[6]

3. *Federal funding for social and public housing*

Neoliberal ideologies have promoted placing responsibility for housing on local governments, the private sector, or service providers, absolving the federal government of responsibility for funding new and existing affordable housing. With concrete federal resources, communities could address maintenance backlogs, build new safe and accessible housing, and create community-based solutions to move people from waitlists into safe homes.

4. *Reparations*

Specific funds and resources (including land and housing) should be given to Indigenous peoples and descendants of enslaved people who have historically been excluded from access to safe and secure housing. Settlers have profited from stolen lands where houses now sit. These forms of extraction are the foundation for contemporary wealth inequality.

5. *Abolitionist planning*

Abolition movements underscore the inability of reformist approaches to address institutional inequality. Abolitionist planning not only critiques technocratic planning in neoliberal societies but questions the ability of institutionalized planning to address challenges and/or inequality while working within the very institutions that create structural inequality. Stefano Harney and Fred Moten's manifesto, *The Undercommoms: Fugitive Planning and Black Study*, offers an alternative conceptualization of bureaucratic planning. Planning in the undercommons resists the limitations of planning and policy that appear in the pages of this book; or, as they describe, "planning in the undercommons is not an activity, not fishing or dancing or teaching or loving, but the ceaseless experiment with the future presence of the forms of life that make such activities possible."[7] Radical possibilities emerge from planning in the under-commons that might move us beyond the limited top-down frameworks of revitalization that are positioned as the progressive way to address past planning failures.

A housing guarantee, guaranteed basic income, public funding for social and public housing, and reparations would need to be paired with much broader societal changes, including free and accessible child care, transit, food accessibility, and health care (including elder care). Further, while policy interventions are one concrete way to address precarity and disparity, they are limited because the *very* institutions where these policies are enacted created the problems in the first place. As former Regent Park resident Chandra noted, there is abundant potential in community ownership and community-led transformation. After all, residents are not in need of anyone telling them what their community needs, what the community's strengths are, or what problems they face. It is residents who are best suited to lead and construct sustainable and thriving communities. In Toronto, leading organizations that have long fought for housing justice and social supports include Association of Community Organizations for Reform Now (ACORN) Canada, Advocacy Centre for Tenants Ontario, Colour of Poverty, Income Security Advocacy Centre, National Aboriginal Housing Association, Ontario Coalition Against Poverty (OCAP), Sistering, Tenants for Social Housing, Workers Action Centre, Regent Park Coalition, and many more. These organizations have paved and continue to pave the way toward a more just future. We would be best served by following their lead.

Urban Possibilities

REVITALIZE, v. trans. To restore to vitality; to put new life or vigour into.
—Oxford English Dictionary and Thesaurus[8]

Precarious Constructions explores urban revitalization processes as a window into broader questions about social regulation and the ways that racism, classism, and exclusion are foundational to liberal democratic societies. Looking closely at the revitalization of two public housing projects in Toronto, I examine how purported efforts to integrate immigrants, "culturally diverse groups," and segregated neighborhoods actually limit equity and can (re)produce ethnoracial and class hierarchies and precarity.

A construction is built based on blueprints, established methods, and logics. Constructions, as such, are flexible and adaptable. Because constructions are not natural or neutral, there is space for contestation and change. And when we deconstruct what we otherwise might take for granted, new insights emerge and new possibilities become visible. One of the main aims of this book is to dig into the taken-for-granted constructions of diversity, surveillance, and consultation mobilized via neoliberal multiculturalism. The revitalization plans employ these constructions as evidence of efforts that support the liberal tenets of integration and inclusion. What becomes clear, however, is that celebrating diversity is not antiracism, surveillance does not equate to safety, and consultation does not require impactful participation or the implementation of residents' ideas. Urban revitalization is not the only framework for providing affordable housing. The term "revitalize" is defined as breathing new life into something or the restoration of vitality. Yet, as residents asserted, Regent Park and Lawrence Heights were in fact thriving and vibrant communities that were, and continue to be, full of life. Deconstruction therefore allows us to excavate the buried, unstable, and misleading assumptions embedded in revitalization logics that obscure power dynamics at play and limit what we imagine as possible.

Notes

Introduction

1. Laura Murray, "Sir John A. Macdonald: Nation Builder or Racist?," *Toronto Star*, January 9, 2015.

2. Confederation refers to the federal union of three British North American colonies (Nova Scotia, New Brunswick, and the Province of Canada) and the formation of the Dominion of Canada. The British Parliament voted on confederation in 1867 resulting in the passing of the British North America Act.

3. The Chinese Head Tax (1885) was a fee charged to Chinese peoples arriving in Canada to discourage immigration from China after the Canadian Pacific Railroad was completed (as Chinese laborers were recruited as the key labor source in railroad construction). It was abolished in 1923; in the 1940s, a delegation of South African officials visited Canada to learn about the "success" of Canada's segregationist reserve system to inform their vision of apartheid.

4. Ian Austen, "Canada, Too, Faces Reckoning with History and Racism," *New York Times*, August 28, 2016.

5. "Construction," Merriam-Webster Dictionary, https://www.merriam-webster .com/dictionary/construction. Accessed May 5, 2023.

6. Lefebvre, *Production of Space*; Soja, *Thirdspace*; Razack, *Race, Space*.

7. For more on precarity and urban policies, see Gilbert, Khosla, and De Jong, "Precaritization and Urban Growth."

8. Foucault, "Discipline," 32–33.

9. Burr, "Regent Park Revitalization."

10. Regent Park Collaborative Team, *Regent Park Revitalization Study*, 35.

11. Purdy, "Building Homes"; Sewell, *Houses and Homes*; Sharma, *Home Economics*.

12. Hulchanski, "What Factors," 222.

13. Purdy, "Building Homes"; Purdy, "'Ripped Off'"; Purdy, "Scaffolding Citizenship."

14. Purdy, "Building Homes"; Purdy, "Scaffolding Citizenship."

15. Sharma, *Home Economics*, 7.

16. Yuval-Davis, *Gender and Nation*.

17. Maynard, *Policing Black Lives*, 4.

18. Thobani, *Exalted Subjects*.

19. Thobani, *Exalted Subjects*, 19.

20. Chatterjee, *The Nation and Its Fragments*.

21. Hall, "Conclusion," 209.

22. Kymlicka, "Rise and Fall?"

23. Gutmann, *Multiculturalism*.

24. Gutmann, *Multiculturalism*, 3.

25. Mackey, *House of Difference*, 63–64.

26. Mackey, *House of Difference*.

27. Mackey, *House of Difference*, 62.

28. Kymlicka, *Multicultural Citizenship*; Mackey, *House of Difference*.

29. Kymlicka, *Theory and Practice*, 21–22.

30. Mackey, *House of Difference*, 67.

31. Mills, *Black Rights/White Wrongs*, 12.

32. Bannerji, *Dark Side*; Goonewardena and Kipfer, "Spaces of Difference"; Mackey, *House of Difference*; Razack, Smith, and Thobani, *States of Race*; Thobani, *Exalted Subjects*.

33. Melamed, "Spirit of Neoliberalism," 7.

34. Kymlicka, *Multicultural Citizenship*; Taylor, *Multiculturalism and Politics*; also, Bannerji, *Dark Side*; Mackey, *House of Difference*; McCready, "Redressing Redress"; Modood, *Multiculturalism*; Povinelli, *Cunning of Recognition*; Teelucksingh, *Claiming Space*; Thobani, *Exalted Subjects*.

35. Alibhai-Brown, *After Multiculturalism*; see also Mackey, *House of Difference*; Dávila, *Barrio Dreams*; Teelucksingh, *Claiming Space*.

36. Bannerji, *Dark Side*; Mackey, *House of Difference*; Razack, *Race, Space*; Thobani, *Exalted Subjects*.

37. Mackey, *House of Difference*; Thobani, *Exalted Subjects*.

38. Berrey, "Divided over Diversity"; Jacobs, *Edge of Empire*.

39. Day, *Alien Capital*, 168.

40. McCready, "Redressing Redress," 166.

41. Jacobs, *Life and Death*.

42. Burayidi, *Cities*; Fainstein, "Cities and Diversity"; Fincher and Iveson, *Planning and Diversity*.

43. For more on planning and neoliberalism: Campbell, Tait, and Watkins, "Is There Space?"

44. For more on diversity and equity and urban planning: Ashley, Loh, Bubb, and Durham, "Diversity, Equity, and Inclusion"; Loh and Kim, "Are We Planning?"; American Planning Association, *Planning for Equity*; Israel and Frenkel, "Social Justice"; Manaugh, Badami, and El-Geneidy, "Integrating Social Equity"; Campbell, Tait, and Watkins, "Is There Space?"; Meerow, Pajouhesh, and Miller, "Social Equity"; and Metzger, "Theory and Practice."

45. Keil and Kipfer, "Toronto Inc?"; Slater, "Gentrification in Canada's Cities"; Bradford, "Placing Social Policy?"; Hackworth, "The Durability"; Keil. "'Common-Sense' Neoliberalism"; Hackworth and Moriah, "Neoliberalism, Contingency"; Hulchanski and Shapcott, *Finding Room*.

46. Harvey, *A Brief History*, 3.

47. Brenner and Theodore, "Cities and the Geographies," 103.

48. Peck and Tickell, "Neoliberalizing Space," 384; see also Brenner and Theodore, "Cities and the Geographies"; Wilson, "Toward a Contingent," 772.

49. Dávila, *Barrio Dreams*; Slater, "Gentrification in Canada's Cities."

50. Lees, Slater, and Wyly, *Gentrification*, 137. For more on gentrification and state involvement, see Lees, Slater, and Wyly, *Gentrification*; and Hackworth and Smith, "Changing State."

51. Hackworth and Smith, "Changing State," 464; see Slater, "Gentrification in Canada's Cities," for an in-depth analysis of gentrification in the Canadian context.

52. Glass, *London: Aspects of Change*.

53. Smith, *New Urban Frontier*.

54. Smith, *New Urban Frontier*, 32.

55. Smith, "Gentrification and Uneven Development," 139.

56. Smith, "Toward a Theory of Gentrification."

57. Shaw, "Gentrification," 2.

58. Smith, "New Globalism, New Urbanism," 338.

59. The phrase "white-painting" refers to gentrified homes in Toronto that were purchased by middle-class residents and often painted white (Slater, "Gentrification in Canada's Cities," 42).

60. Atkinson and Bridge, *Gentrification*, 5.

61. Both feminist and antiracist analyses provide insight into the uneven gendered and racialized effects of processes of gentrification. The displacement of communities of color not only dispossesses people of property, but it deprives people of civic connections created through employment, cultural networks, places of worship, schools, and so forth. The displacement caused by gentrification often moves low-income and racially stigmatized populations away from important social networks such as childcare and community services, further marginalizing already historically excluded social groups. Additionally, communities racialized as nonwhite that live in a downtown core, in areas such as Regent Park, or in close proximity to transit lines, are often pushed out by gentrification to the peripheries of cities, where there is less public infrastructure and limited employment opportunities. My research does not focus on displacement but instead examines how residents are "kept" in place. This is not to say that there was no displacement, despite the insistence on the right of return. However, I do not track displacement in this book. For more on displacement in Regent Park, see Johnson and Johnson, *Regent Park Redux*, chapter 6. In Lawrence Heights, because of successful tenant advocacy, Toronto Community Housing Corporation has committed to zero displacement.

62. Smith, "New Globalism, New Urbanism," 445.

63. Smith, "New Globalism, New Urbanism"; Warton, "Gentrification."

64. Toews, *Stolen City*; Woods, *Development Arrested*.

65. Toews, *Stolen City*; Coulthard, *Red Skin, White Masks*.

66. For a discussion of the relationship between racial capitalism and settler colonialism in the context of another Canadian city, Winnipeg, see Toews, *Stolen City*.

67. Toews, *Stolen City*, 22.

68. Valverde, *Everyday Law*; Teelucksingh, *Claiming Space*; Boudreau, Keil, and Young, *Changing Toronto*; Hackworth, "The Durability"; Kipfer and Keil, "Toronto Inc?"

69. Regent Park Collaborative Team, *Regent Park Revitalization Study*, 5. The phrase "eyes on the street" references a concept Jane Jacobs developed in *Life and Death*.

70. "Newcomers" is a common term used in official documents to refer to new immigrants in Canada.

71. Dan Levin, "In Toronto, a Neighborhood in Despair Transforms into a Model of Inclusion," *New York Times*, February 28, 2016.

72. MacDonald, "Aboriginal Peoples."

73. Sharma, *Home Economics*, 7.

Chapter One

1. Madden and Marcuse, *In Defense of Housing*, 4.

2. Purdy, "Building Homes, Building Citizens."

3. Rose, *Regent Park*.

4. Carver, "Memorandum on Regent Park."

5. Roberts and Sykes, *Urban Regeneration*, 18.

6. See Pickett, "Urban Renewal in Canada"; Carter, "Neighborhood Improvement," 10.

7. Regent Park was called Cabbagetown until the construction of the public housing neighborhood. The gentrification of Donvale in the 1960s led to the reassignment of the moniker (Caulfield, *City Form*, 21–22).

8. City of Toronto, Bylaw No. 17080.

9. Rose, *Canadian Housing Policies*. Voters previously rejected efforts to address poor housing conditions and renewal in 1937 (Johnson and Johnson, *Regent Park Redux*, 12).

10. Purdy, "'Ripped Off,'" 56.

11. Zapparoli, *Regent Park*, 16.

12. Purdy, "'Ripped Off,'" 46.

13. Purdy, "'Ripped Off.'"

14. *Globe and Mail*, "Former Metro Planner Says Public Housing a 'Ridiculous Giveaway,'" March 2, 1956.

15. *Globe and Mail*, "Public Housing a 'Ridiculous Giveaway.'"

16. Toronto, *Canada's Redevelopment*.

17. Regent Park Collaborative Team, *Regent Park Revitalization Study*.

18. For more on the history of Regent Park, see Johnson and Johnson, *Regent Park Redux*; Rose, *Canadian Housing Policies*; Purdy, "'Ripped Off'"; Purdy, "Building Homes, Building Citizens."

19. City of Toronto, *Lawrence-Allen Revitalization Plan*.

20. City of Toronto, *Lawrence-Allen Revitalization Plan*, 3.

21. Rose, *Governing Metropolitan Toronto*, 70.

22. Rose, *Governing Metropolitan Toronto*.

23. City of Toronto, *Lawrence-Allen Revitalization Plan*, 5.

24. Sterling and Cappe, *Lawrence Heights*.

25. Because of Lawrence Heights' unique location and a design that is not in the form of blocks, like in Regent Park, the boundary is more circular and in some cases does not exactly align with these street boundaries.

26. Toronto Community Housing Corporation, "Backgrounder: Lawrence Heights Revitalization."

27. Downsview Airport, built in 1929, was used to test planes until it was expanded and used by the Canadian Air Force until 1996. It was not a commercial airport.

28. Kipfer and Petrunia, "Recolonization and Public Housing," 114.

29. Kipfer and Petrunia, "Recolonization and Public Housing," 114.

30. Kipfer and Petrunia, "Recolonization and Public Housing."

31. Purdy, "'Ripped Off,'" 107.

32. Lees, Slater, and Wyly, *Gentrification*.

33. Anderson, *Vancouver's Chinatown*; Nelson, "Space of Africville." However, this was not the case for the redevelopment of the old Cabbagetown or the greenfield project of Lawrence Heights, both located in Toronto.

34. Purdy, "'Ripped Off.'"

35. Goldberg, *Racist Culture*, 188.

36. Hackworth and Moriah, "Roll-Out Neoliberalism."

37. This history has been well-documented: Hackworth, "Roll-Out Neoliberalism"; Hackworth and Moriah, "Neoliberalism, Contingency,"; Keil and Kipfer, "Toronto Inc?"

38. In Canada, social housing and public housing are often used interchangeably. However, public housing in Canada is housing built with public funds and managed by an agent of the state. Social housing can be managed by the private sector or NGOs but might receive support from government programs, etc., to subsidize rent. TCHC uses both terms when referring to its housing stock. THC offers subsidized, affordable, and market rate units.

39. Hulchanski, *Housing Policy*, 9.

40. Harris quoted in Hackworth, "Roll-Out Neoliberalism," 13.

41. Hackworth and Moriah, "Neoliberalism, Contingency," 515.

42. Hackworth and Moriah, "Neoliberalism, Contingency."

43. Hackworth, "Roll-Out Neoliberalism," 18.

44. Hackworth and Moriah, "Neoliberalism, Contingency," 518.

45. Hackworth and Moriah, "Neoliberalism, Contingency," 518.

46. Hackworth and Moriah, "Neoliberalism, Contingency."

47. Hackworth and Moriah, "Neoliberalism, Contingency," 515.

48. City of Toronto, 2023.

49. City of Toronto, "Toronto Community Housing."

50. Scandals affecting TCHC include incidents of fraud, kickbacks for contracts, the selling of units, and its public-private partnerships that enrich private developers with questionable advantage to the public good.

51. Horak and Moore, "Policy Shift."

52. Horak and Moore, "Policy Shift," 206.

53. Miraftab, "Trojan Horse."

54. Talwar Kapoor, *Understanding What Matters*.

55. Talwar Kapoor, *Understanding What Matters*.

56. For more on the Regent Park revitalization planning process see Johnson and Johnson, *Regent Park Redux*.

57. The low-income cutoff, or LICO, is the measurement or indicator used in Canada for low income.

58. Toronto Community Housing Corporation, "Annual Review 2004," 10.

59. Toronto Community Housing Corporation, "Annual Review 2002," 10.

60. Toronto Community Housing Corporation, "Rent: Subsidized Housing."

61. Toronto Community Housing Corporation, *Report on Regent Park*, 30.

62. Regent Park Collaborative Team, *Regent Park Revitalization Study*, 2002.

63. Toronto Community Housing Corporation, *Report on Regent Park*, 30.

64. Toronto Community Housing Corporation, "Annual Review 2004," 10.

65. Regent Park Collaborative Team, *Regent Park Revitalization Study*, 8.

66. Horak and Moore, "Policy Shift," 194.

67. Johnson and Johnson, *Regent Park Redux*, 5.

68. Johnson and Johnson, *Regent Park Redux*, 5.

69. *Spacing*, "Regent Park Revitalization," December 7, 2021. http://spacing.ca /toronto/2021/12/07/regent-park-revitalization-a-progress-report-by-spacing/

70. City of Toronto, "Implementing Tenants First," 2.

71. City of Toronto, 2016 Neighborhood Profiles, 72.

72. According to the *Lawrence-Allen Revitalization Plan*, "Investment is particularly important in Lawrence-Allen because the area lies within the Lawrence Heights Priority Neighborhood, one of thirteen priority neighborhoods designated by the city council and targeted for improvements in physical and social infrastructure. The revitalization plan is a tool to understand and plan for these improvements and an opportunity to ensure that the new community will be livable, by providing for an appropriate range of social infrastructure that supports both the existing and future population (City of Toronto, *Lawrence-Allen Revitalization Plan*, 7).

73. Accurate data on the population of Lawrence Heights is difficult to obtain. The neighborhood is split into two census tracts; those census tracts are shared with the neighboring communities as well. Even the city neighborhood profiles of Lawrence Heights include an entire ward profile that covers multiple census tracts.

74. Data on the current median incomes is not available.

75. I explore the meaning of this neighborhood nickname in chapter 4.

76. For example see "Just Desserts Case Developed into Strange Trip for All Involved," *Globe and Mail*, May 1, 1999; "Police See Rise of Violent Interference in Arrests: 'It's a Sign of the Times,' Officer Says of Mob Attack in Which Nine Metro Toronto Officers Hurt," *Globe and Mail*, November 22, 1995; "The Lowdown on the Heights Neighborhoods/Residents of a Poor Community with a Reputation for Crime Want to Lay the Stereotypes to Rest," *Globe and Mail*, April 26, 1994; "Don't Blame Me; Work With Me: Black Community Is Not to Blame for Just Desserts Shooting," *Toronto Star*, April 19, 1994; "Crime Increase Worries Public Housing Authority," *Toronto Star*, January 18, 1994; "Lawrence Heights Residents Object to CMHC Plan," *Toronto Star*, July 12, 1990; "Hard Keeping Lid on Bold Housing Experiment: Stress, Decay, Crime Frustrate Policy to House People in Direst Need," *Toronto Star*, November 20, 1990; "Housing Authority Loses Bid to Evict Drug Dealer's Mother," *Globe and Mail*, February 12, 1988; "Pushers Ousted from Public Housing: 65 Families Linked to Drug Dealing," *Toronto Star*, October 17, 1988; "150 Angry Blacks Crowd Meeting to Denounce Treatment by Police Community 'in State of Siege' after Police Arrest 10 in Sweep," *Toronto Star*, October 30, 1986; "Flatten Park's Hills Used as Hideouts, Yorkdale Group Asks," *Globe and Mail*, July 24, 1984; "Racial Tension Prompts Move," *Globe and Mail*, July 19, 1984.

77. Some argue that the nickname comes from the 1950s movie *The Asphalt Jungle*.

78. "Don't Blame Me; Work with Me," *Toronto Star*, April 19, 1994; "Crime Increase Worries," *Toronto Star*, January 18, 1994.

79. City of Toronto, "Report: Affordable Housing."

80. City of Toronto, "Report: Affordable Housing," 1.

81. City of Toronto, *Lawrence-Allen Emerging*, 1.

82. City of Toronto, *Lawrence-Allen Emerging*.

83. City of Toronto, *Lawrence-Allen Revitalization*, 1.

84. City of Toronto, *Lawrence-Allen Revitalization*, 2.

85. City of Toronto, "Report: Affordable Housing"; City of Toronto, *Lawrence-Allen Emerging*; City of Toronto, *Lawrence-Allen Revitalization*.

86. CBC, "TCHC Repair Backlog Will Require Tax Increase, Coun Perks Says." April 1, 2015. www.cbc.ca/news/canada/toronto/tchc-repair-backlog-will-require-tax-increase-coun-perks-says-1.3017417.

87. Social Planning Toronto, *Toronto: Good, Bad, Ugly*.

88. Victoria Gibson, "More Than 81,000 Households Are Waiting for Subsidized Housing in Toronto," *Toronto Star*, January 19, 2021.

89. Laurie Monsebraaten, "Ontario's Affordable Housing Wait List Grows," *Toronto Star*, May 25, 2016.

90. City of Toronto, "Toronto to Transfer TCHC's."

91. City of Toronto, "Implementing Tenants First,"10; the city identified the main reason for this shift as a result of the outdated and unsustainable original TCHC block subsidy funding model (City of Toronto, "Implementing Tenants First").

92. Toronto Foundation, *Vital Signs 2021 Report*.

93. Toronto Foundation, *Vital Signs 2019 Report*, 12.

94. Toronto Public Health, "Unequal City," 7.

95. Toronto Foundation, *Vital Signs 2019 Report*, 22.

96. Toronto Foundation, *Vital Signs 2019 Report*, 22.

97. Toronto Foundation, *Vital Signs 2019 Report*, 23.

98. United Way, *Opportunity Equation*, 15

99. Canada Mortgage and Housing Corporation, "Housing Market Information Portal."

100. Canadian Center for Economic Analysis and Canadian Urban Institute, "Toronto Housing Market Analysis," 53. For more on housing affordability in Toronto, see Walks, "Global City," 130-144.

101. Royal Bank of Canada, "Housing Trends."

102. Horak and Moore, "Policy Shift," 183–184.

Chapter Two

1. Doucet, *Anatomy Urban Legend*; Teelucksingh, *Claiming Space*; Valverde "Ethic of Diversity"; Valverde, *Everyday Law*.

2. Toronto Community Housing Corporation, *Regent Social Development, Part I*, 1.

3. Abu-Laban and Gabriel, *Selling Diversity*; Ahmed, *On Being Included*; Berrey, *Enigma of Diversity*; Valverde, *Everyday Law*.

4. Berrey, *Enigma of Diversity*; Valverde, *Everyday Law*.

5. Bell and Hartmann, "Diversity in Everyday Discourse"; Berrey, *Enigma of Diversity*; Blommaert and Verschueren, *Debating Diversity*; Bonilla-Silva, *Racism without*

Racists; Michaels, *Trouble with Diversity*; Smelser and Alexander, *Diversity and Its Discontents*.

6. Ahmed, *On Being Included*, 14.

7. Dose and Klimoski refer to a "diversity of diversity" in their research on work values ("Diversity of Diversity"). Vertovec references the "diversification of diversity" in relation to his work on superdiversity, where he explores how rates of diversity in particular contexts are increasing due to migration and immigration, in combination with other factors ("Super-Diversity and Its Implications").

8. Dan Levin, "In Toronto, a Neighborhood in Despair Transforms into a Model of Inclusion," *New York Times*, February 28, 2016.

9. Levin, "In Toronto."

10. Regent Park Collaborative Team, *Regent Park Revitalization Study*, 5.

11. Regent Park Collaborative Team, *Regent Park Revitalization Study*.

12. Regent Park Collaborative Team, *Regent Park Revitalization Study*, 34.

13. Toronto Community Housing Corporation, "Regent Park Revitalization Phase One Groundbreaking." Toronto: Toronto Community Housing Corporation, 2007. www.torontohousing.ca/News/Whatsnew/Pages/RegentparkrevitalizationphaseOne condominiumgroundbreaking.Aspx

14. Toronto Community Housing Corporation, "Regent Park Community Update," 17.

15. This concern is ongoing and currently being addressed by the Regent Park Coalition.

16. Interview with Chandra, September 23, 2010.

17. Toronto Community Housing Corporation, "Regent Park Revitalization Phase One Groundbreaking," Toronto: Toronto Community Housing Corporation, 2007. www.torontohousing.ca/News/Whatsnew/Pages/RegentparkrevitalizationphaseOne condominiumgroundbreaking.Aspx

18. Interview with Andrea, September 30, 2010.

19. Jennifer Pagliaro, "Regent Park Residents Say They Can't Access Their Neighbourhood Pool: City Data Backs Them Up." *Toronto Star*, February 2, 2019.

20. Pagliaro, "Regent Park Residents"; See Pitter, "Reconsidering Revitalization," for an important discussion around access regarding the Regent Park revitalization from the perspective of a former resident/current community worker.

21. Interview with Andrea, September 30, 2010.

22. Kipfer and Petrunia, "Recolonization and Public Housing," 111.

23. I am not suggesting that a bank and an affordable grocery store were not important additions to Parliament Street as the community did not previously have a local bank or large grocery store. Other possibilities include a local credit union or grocery cooperatives.

24. August, "Revitalisation Gone Wrong"; August and Walks, "Social Mix"; DeFilippis and Fraser, "Why Do We Want?"; Joseph, Chaskin, and Webber, "Theoretical Basis"; Vale and Shamsuddin, "All Mixed Up."

25. Joseph, Chaskin, and Webber, "Theoretical Basis."

26. August, "Revitalisation Gone Wrong"; August, "Canadian Public Housing"; Chaskin and Joseph, "Social Interaction"; Lees, "Gentrification and Social Mixing"; Joseph, Chaskin, and Webber, "Theoretical Basis."

27. Chaskin and Joseph, "Social Interaction."

28. Additionally, Khare, Joseph, and Chaskin ("Enduring Significance") reference the "enduring significance of race in mixed-income developments" to highlight the impact of racism and perception among middle-income residents who blame individual behavior for their plight and poverty (relying on the historical tropes signalled in endnote 5 of this chapter).

29. Hackworth and Moriah, "Neoliberalism, Contingency."

30. Toronto Community Housing Corporation, *Regent Park Revitalization Initiative*, 5.

31. Toronto Community Housing Corporation, *Regent Park Revitalization Initiative*, 6.

32. Moore and Wright, "Toronto's Market-Oriented"; Toronto Community Housing Corporation, *Partners in Communities*.

33. Regent Park Collaborative Team, *Regent Park Revitalization Study*, 47–48.

34. Interview with Leroy, August 9, 2010.

35. Moore and Wright, "Toronto's Market-Oriented"; Toronto Community Housing Corporation, *Partners in Communities*, 5.

36. Ballentyne in Kipfer and Petrunia, "Recolonization and Public Housing," 123.

37. Moore and Wright, "Toronto's Market-Oriented," 70. See chapter one.

38. Toronto Community Housing Corporation, "Regent Park Update," 8.

39. Toronto Community Housing Corporation, *Regent Social Development, Part I*, 1.

40. Toronto Community Housing Corporation, *Regent Social Development, Part I*.

41. Toronto Community Housing Corporation, *Regent Social Development, Part I*, 22.

42. Toronto Community Housing Corporation, *Regent Social Development, Part I*, 23.

43. Toronto Community Housing Corporation, *Regent Social Development, Part I*.

44. Toronto Community Housing Corporation, *Regent Social Development, Part I*, 22.

45. Interview with Amanda, July 27, 2010.

46. However, what Amanda also highlights is that the transformation will increase property values. Here, there is no analysis of what increased property values means (and has meant) for low-income residents.

47. Kipfer and Petrunia "Recolonization and Public Housing."

48. Kipfer and Petrunia, "Recolonization and Public Housing"; Moore and Wright, "Toronto's Market-Oriented"; Regent Park Collaborative Team, *Regent Park Revitalization Study*.

49. Regent Park Collaborative Team, *Regent Park Revitalization Study*.

50. Laven quoted in the Regent Park Collaborative Team, *Regent Park Revitalization Study*, 77–78.

51. I examine the question of social norms and crime rates in chapter 3.

52. James, "'Slum Clearance' to 'Revitalisation,'" 83.

53. Rowe and Dunn, "Tenure and Mix,"1265.

54. Rowe and Dunn, "Tenure and Mix," 1268–1269.

55. The racist culture of poverty thesis was popularized by Oscar Lewis, who argued that Puerto Ricans and Mexicans, in particular, adapted to poverty that led to a culture of poverty. Traits such as laziness, lack of ambition, dependency, no knowledge of history, disorganization, lack of structure, etc., would be passed down to younger generations, producing a culture of poverty. He argued that a culture of poverty was a way of life. His theory became popular with policy makers and politicians

who used the concept to inform social policy and reports, including the infamous Moynihan report. Lewis, *La Vida*; Lewis, *Five Families*; Spalding, *Race, Class*, 17–18.

56. August, "Revitalisation Gone Wrong."

57. August and Walks, "Social Mix"

58. August and Walks, "Social Mix," 282.

59. Toronto Community Housing Corporation, *Regent Park Executive Summary*, 8.

60. Toronto Community Housing Corporation, *Regent Park Executive Summary*, 23.

61. Regent Park Collaborative Team, *Regent Park Revitalization Study*, 35.

62. Personal Interview with Corinne, September 10, 2010.

63. Teelucksingh, *Claiming Space*, 1.

64. Chaskin and Joseph, "Social Interaction"; DeFilippis and Fraser, "Why Do We Want?"; Joseph and Chaskin, "Mixed-Income Developments."

65. Personal Interview with Corinne, September 10, 2010.

66. Similarly, the *Lawrence-Allen Revitalization Plan* describes, "While culturally diverse, Lawrence Heights has a limited mix of uses and housing types. The neighbourhood lacks good access to services, and the quality of physical infrastructure is poor." (City of Toronto, *Lawrence-Allen Revitalization Plan*, chapter 1, 5.)

67. Kipfer and Petrunia, "Recolonization and Public Housing," 128–129.

Chapter Three

1. Toronto Community Housing Corporation, "Backgrounder," 1.

2. City of Toronto, *Lawrence-Allen Revitalization Plan*.

3. Regent Park Collaborative Team, *Regent Park Revitalization Study*, 2, 31.

4. Davis, *City of Quartz*.

5. Graham, *Cities Under Siege*.

6. Graham, *Cities Under Siege*, 32.

7. Rosenbaum, "Theory and Research"; Schweitzer, Kim, and Mackin, "Impact Built Environment."

8. Jacobs, *Life and Death*, 35.

9. Fennell, *Last Project Standing*, 202.

10. Regent Park Collaborative Team, *Regent Park Revitalization Study*; Toronto Community Housing Corporation, *Regent Social Development, Part I*; City of Toronto, "Staff Report: Lawrence-Allen"; City of Toronto, "Lawrence-Allen Secondary Plan."

11. Newman, *Defensible Space*.

12. Newman *Defensible Space*; Robinson, "Theoretical Development."

13. Cashmore and McLaughlin, *Out of Order*; Galabuzi, *Canada's Economic Apartheid*; James, "Up to No Good"; Tator and Henry, *Racial Profiling*; Young, *Marginalized Black Men*.

14. Maynard, *Policing Black Lives*.

15. Maynard, *Policing Black Lives*, 51.

16. Maynard, *Policing Black Lives*, 123.

17. Toronto Community Housing Corporation, *Regent Social Development, Part I*, 12.

18. Regent Park Collaborative Team, *Regent Park Revitalization Study*, 8.

19. Interview with Nick, August 5, 2010.

20. Johnson and Johnson, *Regent Park Redux*, 43.

21. City of Toronto, "Lawrence-Allen Secondary Plan," 16.

22. City of Toronto, "Staff Report: Lawrence-Allen," 10.

23. City of Toronto, *Lawrence-Allen Revitalization*, 65.

24. Sterling and Cappe, *Lawrence Heights*, 1.

25. City of Toronto, "Regent Park Secondary," 1.

26. Sterling and Cappe, *Lawrence Heights*.

27. Interview with Nick, August 5, 2010.

28. For example, Nick claimed, "It is when you get neighborhoods that don't have well designed spaces, spaces that are not well used, people feel marginalized and you get these issues. So, you can go down to a detailed perspective and say well we need better lighting here and where are routes of escape if someone is suddenly assaulted in the park how do they get away, you know you can get to that level of detail but fundamentally I think you have to take it up a step and take a broader perspective on it. . . . So you give them a strong sense of community to . . . those are all things that contribute to safe communities."

29. Regent Park Collaborative Team, *Regent Park Revitalization Study*, 5, 67.

30. Laven quoted in Regent Park Collaborative Team, *Regent Park Revitalization Study*, 77–78.

31. Safety and security are not necessarily distinctly Canadian (other countries highlight the strength of their militaries or low rates of crime and violence) but in this context are constructed as aligning with values of inclusion and integration alongside Canadian multiculturalism.

32. Greg said, "The ever popular . . . whatever it is called . . . through environmental design . . . I forget the actual word." Vanessa: "CPTED?" Greg: "Yes. The acronym is CPTED and is something . . . through environmental design. So, there is going to be a lot of that. There is going to be 'eyes on the street'; there is not going to be places where somebody can run from one side to the other and not be seen. So, um, I do believe that certain things will be curtailed. Now, if people think that it is going to go away completely, they have lost their mind because it is all over."

33. Khenti, "Canadian War"; Roberts, *Crime, Race, and Reproduction*.

34. Chandra said, "There is a perception that there is a linkage between the level of a neighborhood's income and the level of crime."

35. Interview with Eva, September 21, 2010.

36. Interview with Sheila, September 22, 2010.

37. Interview with Eva, September 21, 2010.

38. Interview with Sheila, September 22, 2010.

39. Interview with Sheila, September 22, 2010.

40. Neptune is a TCHC property just north of Lawrence Heights. Many TCHC documents address Lawrence Heights and Neptune in tandem. According to TCHC, "Although 135 to 155 Neptune Drive will not undergo a physical transformation as part of the Lawrence Heights Revitalization, residents are included in many of the social events and will benefit from all the economic opportunities provided through this revitalization project." There is a history of conflict between residents of Neptune

and Lawrence Heights. There were multiple efforts made during the revitalization and consultation process to appropriately and safely consider the concerns of residents about attending meetings in different locations because of potential tensions between residents at meetings, etc. (Toronto Community Housing Corporation, "New Basketball Court Builds Community in Neptune." Toronto: Toronto Community Housing Corporation, 2015. Accessed February 10, 2021. www.torontohousing .ca/news/whatsnew/ pages/new-basketball-court-builds-community-in-neptune.aspx).

41. "Revitalization is not necessarily going to fix those things without some other options. Why are kids selling drugs? Well I'm not justifying anything, but if they really can't get jobs, and they need money, unfortunately we live in a society where that is an option. You know what I mean? They're dropping out of school earlier because they don't necessarily have the support or the willingness to learn in spaces that are hostile, realistically they are hostile. And if there are no productive programs or a lack of things that they need so that they can actually become good citizens, then we had kind of left them to fend for themselves."

42. Interview with Tamia, November 30, 2010.

43. Fanon, *Black Skin, White Masks*; Flint, *Spaces of Hate*; Goldberg, *Threat of Race*; Saberi, "'Paris Problem'"; Maynard, *Policing Black Lives*.

44. Interview with Tamia, November 30, 2010.

45. Interview with Tamia, November 30, 2010.

46. Flint, *Spaces of Hate*; Goldberg, *Threat of Race*.

47. Interview with Chandra, September 23, 2010.

48. In 2012 Pam McConnell was accused of having a conflict of interest because she, along with a large number of other powerful stakeholders, purchased condos in the first private condo building in Regent Park—before a majority of Regent Park residents were relocated back to the community).

49. Residents did not specify what they meant by retaliation. However, based on context, I interpreted their reference to retaliation to signal that if they reported something to the police, the accused or others would harm them for working with the police.

50. Field notes, November 4, 2010.

51. Saberi, "'Paris Problem,'" 51.

52. Interview with Tamia, November 30, 2010.

Chapter Four

1. Interview with Diana, October 7, 2011.

2. Statistics Canada, 2006 Census.

3. Toronto Community Housing Corporation, *Regent Social Development, Part I*, 21.

4. Pateman, *Participation and Democratic Theory*.

5. Arnstein, "Ladder of Citizen Participation."

6. Chambers, "Origins and Practice"; Chambers, "Participation Farmer-Owned."

7. Hickey and Mohan, *Participation*, 5.

8. Chambers, "Origins and Practice"; Chambers, "Participation Farmer-Owned."

9. Forester, *Critical Theory*; Forester, *Planning in the Face*; Healy, "Communicative Turn"; Healey, *Collaborative Planning*; Innes, "Planning Theory's Emerging Paradigm"; see Westin, "Framing of Power," for a review of communicative planning theory.

10. Purcell, "Resisting Neoliberalization."

11. Chaskin, Khare, and Joseph "Participation, Deliberation," 865.

12. Cooke and Kothari, *Participation*, 6

13. Hickey and Mohan, *Participation*, 17.

14. Hickey and Mohan, *Participation*.

15. Cooke and Kothari, *Participation*.

16. Taylor, "Insights into Participation," 125.

17. Ontario Planning Act; for a thorough case study of another consultation project in Toronto, see Valverde, "A Tale of Two."

18. Meagher and Boston, *Community Engagement*, 32.

19. Regent Park Collaborative Team, *Regent Park Revitalization Study*.

20. Regent Park Collaborative Team, *Regent Park Revitalization Study*.

21. Meagher and Boston, *Community Engagement*.

22. Meagher and Boston, *Community Engagement*, 11.

23. Meagher and Boston, *Community Engagement*.

24. Meagher and Boston, *Community Engagement*, 23.

25. Meagher and Boston, *Community Engagement*, 22.

26. Meagher and Boston, *Community Engagement*, 26.

27. Meagher and Boston, *Community Engagement*, 9.

28. Meagher and Boston, *Community Engagement*, 16.

29. Meagher and Boston, *Community Engagement*, 18.

30. Meagher and Boston, *Community Engagement*.

31. Meagher and Boston, *Community Engagement*, 19.

32. Meagher and Boston, *Community Engagement*.

33. Meagher and Boston, *Community Engagement*, 5.

34. Meagher and Boston, *Community Engagement*, 9.

35. Meagher and Boston, *Community Engagement*, 26.

36. Meagher and Boston, *Community Engagement*, 5.

37. Toronto Community Housing Corporation, "Lawrence Heights: Past Events."

38. City of Toronto, "Staff Report: Lawrence-Allen," 5.

39. City of Toronto, "Staff Report: Affordable Housing."

40. Sterling and Cappe, *Lawrence Heights*, 11.

41. Smith, "What Housing Practitioners Can Learn."

42. City of Toronto, *Lawrence Social Development*.

43. Smith, "What Housing Practitioners Can Learn." It is unclear how residents' ranking of applicants were incorporated into the decision-making process.

44. Interview with Aliyyah, October 5, 2010.

45. Toronto Community Housing Corporation, "Regent Community Planning"; Toronto Community Housing Corporation, "Lawrence Community Priorities [Draft]."

46. Interview with Marina, August 3, 2010.

47. Kapoor, "Participatory Development."

48. Informal communication, Marcia, October 28, 2010. Marcia was the director of a local engagement organization in Lawrence Heights.

49. Interview with Tamia, November 30, 2010.

50. Interview with Greg, December 16, 2010.

51. In the 1980s, residents successfully mobilized around funding for a resident-led community center (City of Toronto, "Regent Park Legacy Funds").

52. Toronto Community Housing Corporation, *Regent Social Development, Part I*, 13.

53. Interview with Nick, August 5, 2010.

54. Interview with Aliyyah, October 5, 2010.

55. Interview with Diana, October 7, 2011.

56. Interview with Tamia, November 30, 2010.

57. Interview with Andrea, September 30, 2010.

58. Interview with Benjamin, November 12, 2010.

59. Interview with Aliyyah, October 5, 2010.

60. Interview with Eva, September 21, 2010.

61. Interview with Tamia, November 30, 2010.

62. Interview with Aliyyah, October 5, 2010.

63. Interview with Aliyyah, October 5, 2010.

64. Interview with Benjamin, November 12, 2010.

65. Interview with Benjamin, November 12, 2010.

66. Interview with Diana, October 7, 2011.

67. Interview with Benjamin, November 12, 2010.

68. Interview with Chandra, September 23, 2010.

69. Advertising about community consultations included online on the city and TCHC websites, posters, communication from local community organizations, and communication from animators.

70. This is similar to the language used by the social worker who attended the police meeting in Regent Park as examined in chapter 3.

71. Communication with Merhawit, November, 4, 2010.

72. Communication with Merhawit, November, 4, 2010.

73. Interview with Tamia, November 30, 2010.

74. "TCH Tenants: Watch out for Public Interest," *Basics News*, April 10, 2011.

75. Interview with Aliyyah, October 5, 2010.

76. Aliyyah also explained her desire to participate in these terms: "As for me personally, I would prefer, and this is my kind of idealistic way of thinking, I would rather be aware and involved, and in some way voice whatever it is that I think is the right thing to do at that time, so that in the long run I have some bargaining power, whether it is myself or a group of individuals or the entire community, to say that this is what we want for ourselves. And hope that that actually counts for something. So I think . . . what I can sense is that if you don't get involved and you don't say anything, you really have no say, and that is something that I'm learning as well, because I was never the type to go out and vote as much, but I can see how all of these things really, really directly affects everything that you may have or opportunities that you may have living in Toronto and the world in general."

77. Interview with Greg, December 16, 2010.

78. Interview with Chandra, September 23, 2010.

79. Interview with Sheila, September 22, 2010.

80. Quoted in Aparita Bhandri, "How It Feels to Be 'Revitalized,'" *Local*, 4, January 28, 2020. https://thelocal.to/how-it-feels-to-be-revitalized/.

81. Thanks to Radhika Mongia for this phrasing.

82. Personal communication with Merhawit November, 4, 2010; interview with Merhawit, December 2, 2010; interview with Eva, September 21, 2010.

83. Interview with Chandra, September 23, 2010.

Conclusion

1. Four geographic areas make up the City of Toronto: Toronto and East York, Etobicoke York, Scarborough, and North York. Each area's community council holds regular meetings about local planning and neighborhood issues such as traffic or parking. Community councils report to the Toronto City Council.

2. Interview with Tesfaye, September 30, 2010.

3. Ahmed, *On Being Included*, 163

4. Pitter, "Reconsidering Revitalization," 176.

5. Madden and Marcuse, *In Defense of Housing*.

6. Ferdosi, Mcdowell, Lewchuk, and Ross, *Southern Ontario's*.

7. Harney and Moten, *Undercommons*.

8. Accessed April 17, 2023, www-oed-com.proxy.mtholyoke.edu:2443/view/Entry/164905?rskey=O6LjP6&result=1&isAdvanced=false#eid.

Bibliography

Interviews (alphabetical order)

Personal Interview with Aliyyah, October 5, 2010
Personal Interview with Amanda, July 27, 2010
Personal Interview with Ameena, December 20, 2010
Personal Interview with Andrea, September 30, 2010
Personal Interview with Benjamin, November 12, 2010
Personal Interview with Chandra, September 23, 2010
Personal Interview with Corinne, September 10, 2010
Personal Interview with Diana, October 7, 2011
Personal Interview with Eva, September 21, 2010
Personal Interview with Greg, December 16, 2010
Personal Interview with Gurmuu, September 13, 2010
Personal Interview with Leroy, August 9, 2010
Personal Communication with Marcia, October 28, 2010
Personal Interview with Marina, August 3, 2010
Personal Communication with Merhawit, November 4, 2010
Personal Interview with Merhawit, December 2, 2010
Personal Interview with Nick, August 5, 2010
Personal Interview with Sheila, September 22, 2010
Personal Interview with Tamia, November 30, 2010
Personal Interview with Tesfaye, September 30, 2010

Newspapers and Periodicals

Basic News
Canadian Broadcasting Corporation
Globe and Mail
Local
New York Times
Spacing
Toronto Star

Reports and Planning Documents

American Planning Association. *Planning For Equity Policy Guide*. American Planning
    Association, 2019.
Burr, Tom. "Regent Park Revitalization: Building a Great Neighbourhood." Power-
    Point presentation delivered to the TCHC Board of Directors, June 22, 2012.

Canada Mortgage and Housing Corporation, "Housing Market Information Portal." Accessed July 21, 2022. www03.cmhc-schl.gc.ca/hmip-pimh/en/TableMapChart /Table?TableId=2.2.28&GeographyId=2270&GeographyTypeId=3&DisplayAs =Table&GeograghyName=Toronto.

Canadian Center for Economic Analysis and Canadian Urban Institute. "Toronto Housing Market Analysis, 2019." Accessed January 23, 2023. www.toronto.ca /legdocs/mmis/2019/ph/bgrd/backgroundfile-124480.pdf.

Carver, Humphrey. "Memorandum on the Regent Park Housing Project." Toronto: Toronto Reconstruction Council, 1946.

Chisholm, Sharon. *Affordable Housing in Canada's Urban Communities: A Literature Review*. Ottawa: Canada Mortgage and Housing Corporation, 2003.

Doucet, Michael J. *The Anatomy of an Urban Legend: Toronto's Multicultural Reputation*. Joint Centre of Excellence for Research on Immigration and Settlement. Toronto: CERIS, 2001.

Dupuis, Jean. *Federal Housing Policy: A Historical Perspective*. Ottawa: Parliamentary Research Branch, 2003.

Ferdosi, Mohammed, Tom Mcdowell, Wayne Lewchuk, and Stephanie Ross. *Southern Ontario's Basic Income Experience*, 2020. Accessed July 12, 2021. https:// labourstudies.Mcmaster.Ca/Documents/Southern-Ontarios-Basic-Income -Experience.pdf.

Hulchanski, J. David. *Housing Policy for Tomorrow's Cities*. Discussion Paper F 27. Toronto: Canadian Policy Research Network (CPRN), 2002.

Meagher, Sean, and Tony Boston. *Community Engagement and the Regent Park Redevelopment: Community Engagement Team Report, July to December 2002*. Toronto: Public Interest Strategy and Communications, 2003.

Oberlander, H. Peter, and Arthur L. Fallick. *Housing a Nation: The Evolution of Canadian Housing Policy*. Prepared by the Center For Human Settlements, The University of British Columbia for the Canada Mortgage and Housing Corporation, 1992.

Ontario Planning Act. Toronto: Province of Ontario, 1990.

Regent Park Collaborative Team. *Regent Park Revitalization Study*. Submitted to the Toronto Community Housing Corporation by the Regent Park Collaborative Team, 2002.

Royal Bank of Canada, "Housing Trends." Accessed January 23, 2023. https://royal -bank-of-canada-2124.docs.contently.com/v/homebuyer-blues-dreadful -affordability-gets-worse-in-canada.

Smith, Carmen. *What Housing Practitioners Can Learn from Tenant Leadership and Participation at Lawrence Heights*. Toronto: The Maytree Foundation, 2019. https://maytree.com/Stories/Lawrence-Heights.

Social Planning Toronto. *Toronto After a Decade of Austerity: The Good, the Bad, the Ugly*. Toronto: Social Planning Toronto, January 7, 2020. www.socialplanning toronto.org/good_bad_ugly.

Sterling, Mark, and Lorne Cappe. *Lawrence Heights: A Model Neighborhood*. A paper presented at City Futures 2009: An International Conference on Globalism and Urban Change. Madrid, Spain, June 2–6, 2009.

Talwar Kapoor, Garima. *Understanding What Matters: Summary of the Financial Accountability Office's Report—Housing and Homelessness Programs in Ontario.* Toronto: Maytree Foundation, 2021.

Toronto, City of. Bylaw No. 17080. Toronto: City of Toronto, 1947.

———. "Canada's Premier Housing Redevelopment Project." Toronto: City of Toronto, 1972.

———. "Capital Budget Briefing Note Regent Park," February 13, 2019. www .toronto.ca/legdocs/mmis/2019/bu/bgrd/backgroundfile-126642.pdf.

———. "Implementing Tenants First: A New Funding Model for Toronto Community Housing," 2019. www.toronto.ca/legdocs/mmis/2019/ex/bgrd /backgroundfile-139986.pdf.

———. *Lawrence-Allen Emerging Preferred Plan.* Toronto: City of Toronto, 2010.

———. *Lawrence-Allen Revitalization Plan.* Toronto: City of Toronto, 2010. https:// www.toronto.ca/legdocs/mmis/2010/ny/bgrd/backgroundfile-31038.pdf.

———. "Lawrence-Allen Secondary Plan, Official Plan Amendment #162," Toronto: City of Toronto, 2011. www.toronto.ca/legdocs/mmis/2011/ny/bgrd/background file-41803.pdf.

———. *Lawrence Heights Social Development Plan.* Toronto: City of Toronto, Spring 2012. www.toronto.ca/legdocs/mmis/2012/cd/bgrd/backgroundfile-48446.pdf.

———. "Press Release: City of Toronto to Transfer TCHC's Single-Family Housing to Non-Profit Housing Sector," June 25, 2021. www.toronto.ca/news /city-of-toronto-to-transfer-tchcs-single-family-housing-to-non-profit -housing-sector/.

———. "Regent Park Secondary Plan." Toronto: City of Toronto, 2007. Accessed April 17, 2023. www.toronto.ca/wp-content/uploads/2017/11/902b-cp-official -plan-SP-28-RegentPark.pdf.

———. "Report from Deputy City Manager. Implementing Tenants First: TCHC Scattered Portfolio Plan and an Interim Selection Process for Tenant Directors on the TCHC Board." Toronto: City of Toronto, January 12, 2018. www.toronto.ca /legdocs/mmis/2018/ex/bgrd/backgroundfile-110702.pdf.

———. "Staff Report: Lawrence-Allen Revitalization Plan." Toronto: City of Toronto, June 3, 2010. www.toronto.ca/legdocs/mmis/2010/ny/bgrd/backgroundfile -30947.pdf.

———. "Staff Report: Regent Park Legacy Funds." Toronto: City of Toronto, April 3, 2014. www.toronto.ca/legdocs/mmis/2014/cd/bgrd/backgroundfile -68344.pdf.

———. "Staff Report. To: Affordable Housing Committee." Toronto: City of Toronto, May 31, 2007.

———. "Toronto Community Housing." Accessed January 22, 2023. www.toronto .ca/city-government/accountability-operations-customer-service/city -administration/city-managers-office/agencies-corporations/corporations /toronto-community-housing/.

———. "2016 Neighborhood Profiles, Regent Park," 72. Accessed April 19, 2023. www.toronto.ca/ext/sdfa/Neighbourhood%20Profiles/pdf/2016/pdf1/cpa72.pdf.

Toronto Community Housing Corporation. "Backgrounder: Lawrence Heights and Area Revitalization." Toronto: Toronto Community Housing Corporation, June 4, 2008. www.torontohousing.Ca/Events/Documents/Archives/News /4913lawrence%2oheights%2obackgrounder%20-%20june%202008.pdf.

———. "Lawrence Heights Community Priorities Framework [Draft]." Toronto: Toronto Community Housing Corporation, n.d.

———. "Lawrence Heights: Past Events." Toronto: Toronto Community Housing Corporation, 2011.

———. *Partners in Communities: Annual Review 2004*. Toronto: Toronto Community Housing Corporation, 2004.

———. "Regent Park Community Planning Principles." Toronto: Toronto Community Housing Corporation, n.d.

———. "Regent Park Community Update Meeting." Toronto: Toronto Community Housing Corporation, June 28, 2017.

———. "Regent Park Community Update Meeting." Toronto: Toronto Community Housing Corporation, April 19, 2018.

———. *Regent Park Revitalization Initiative, 2150*. Toronto: Toronto Community Housing Corporation, 2004.

———. *Regent Park Social Development Plan: Executive Summary*. Toronto: Toronto Community Housing Corporation, 2007.

———. *Regent Park Social Development Plan, Part I: Context*. Toronto: Toronto Community Housing Corporation, 2007.

———. *Regent Park Social Development Plan, Part II: Best Practices for Social Inclusion in Mixed-Income Communities*. Toronto: Toronto Community Housing Corporation, 2007.

———, "Rent: Subsidized Housing." Accessed January 23, 2022. www.torontohousing .ca/rent/subsidized-housing.

———. *Report on the Regent Park Revitalization Study*. Toronto: Toronto Community Housing Corporation, 2003.

———. *TCH Annual Review 2002*. Toronto: Toronto Community Housing Corporation, 2002.

Toronto Community Housing Corporation, no. 200330. n.d. Toronto: Toronto Community Housing Corporation.

Toronto Foundation. *Toronto's Vital Signs, 2019 Report*. Toronto: Toronto Foundation, 2019. https://torontofoundation.ca/vitalsigns2019/.

———. *Toronto's Vital Signs, 2021 Report*. Toronto: Toronto Foundation, 2021. https:// torontofoundation.ca/vitalsigns2021/.

Toronto Public Health, City of. "The Unequal City in 2015: Income and Health Inequities in Toronto." Toronto: City of Toronto, 2015. www.toronto .ca/wp-content/uploads/2019/10/98bb-Technical-Report-FINAL-PRINT _AODA.pdf.

United Way, Greater Toronto. "The Opportunity Equation." Toronto: United Way, 2019. www.unitedwaygt.org/wpcontent/uploads/2021/10/The_Opportunity _Equation_Report_FINAL_low-res.pdf.

Books, Essays, Articles

Abu-Laban, Yasmeen, and Christina Gabriel. *Selling Diversity: Immigration, Multiculturalism, Employment Equity, and Globalization*. Toronto: University of Toronto Press, 2002.

Ahmed, Sara. *On Being Included: Racism and Diversity in Institutional Life*. Durham, NC: Duke University Press, 2012.

Alibhai-Brown, Yasmin. *After Multiculturalism*. London: Foreign Policy Center, 2000.

Anderson, Kay. *Vancouver's Chinatown: Racial Discourse in Canada, 1875-1980*. Montreal: McGill-Queen's University Press, 1991.

Arnstein, Sherry. "Ladder of Citizen Participation." *Journal of the American Planners* 5, no. 4 (1969): 216-224.

Ashley, Amanda J., Carolyn G. Loh, Karen Bubb, and Leslie Durham. "Diversity, Equity, and Inclusion Practices in Arts and Cultural Planning." *Journal of Urban Affairs* 44, no. 45, (2022): 727-747.

Atkinson, Rowland, and Gary Bridge, eds. *Gentrification in a Global Context: The New Urban Colonialism*. London: Routledge, 2005.

August, Martine. "Revitalisation Gone Wrong: Mixed-Income Public Housing Redevelopment in Toronto's Don Mount Court." *Urban Studies* 53, no. 16 (2016): 3405-3422.

———. "Social Mix and Canadian Public Housing Redevelopment: Experiences in Toronto." *Canadian Journal of Urban Research* 22, no. 1 (2008): 82-99.

———. "Speculating Social Housing: Mixed-Income Public Housing Redevelopment in Regent Park and Don Mount Court." PhD diss., University of Toronto, 2014. https://tspace.library.utoronto.ca/handle/1807/94533.

August, Martine, and Alan Walks. "From Social Mix to Political Marginalisation? The Redevelopment of Toronto's Public Housing and the Dilution of Tenant Organizational Power." In *Mixed Communities: Gentrification By Stealth*, edited by Gary Bridge, Tim Butler, and Loretta Lees, 273-298. Chicago: Policy Press, 2012.

Bannerji, Himani. *The Dark Side of the Nation: Essays on Multiculturalism, Nationalism, and Gender*. Toronto: Canadian Scholars Press, 2000.

Beck, Ulrich. *What Is Globalization?* Cambridge: Polity Press, 2000.

Bell, Joyce, and Douglas Hartmann. "Diversity in Everyday Discourse: The Cultural Ambiguities and Consequences of Happy Talk." *American Sociological Review* 72 (December 2007): 895-914.

Berrey, Ellen C. "Divided over Diversity." *City and Community* 4 (2005): 143-170.

———. *The Enigma of Diversity: The Language of Race and the Limits of Racial Justice*. Chicago: University of Chicago Press, 2015.

Blommaert, Jan, and Jef Verschueren. *Debating Diversity: Analyzing the Discourse of Tolerance*. New York: Routledge, 1998.

Bonilla-Silva, Edward. *Racism Without Racists: Color-Blind Racism and the Persistence of Racial Inequality in the United States*. Lanham, MD: Rowman and Littlefield, 2003.

Boudreau, Julie-Anne, Roger Keil, and Douglas Young. *Changing Toronto: Governing Urban Neoliberalism*. Toronto: University of Toronto Press, 2009.

Bradford, Neil. "Placing Social Policy? Reflections on Canada's New Deal for Cities and Communities." *Canadian Journal of Urban Research* 16, no. 2 (2007): 1–26.

Brenner, Neil, and Nik Theodore. "Cities and the Geographies of 'Actually Existing Neoliberalism.'" *Antipode* 34, no. 3 (2002): 49–79.

Burayidi, Michael A., ed. *Cities and the Politics of Difference: Multiculturalism and Diversity in Urban Planning*. Toronto: University of Toronto Press, 2015.

Bunting, Trudi, Pierre Filion, and Ryan R. Walker, eds. *Canadian Cities in Transition: New Directions in the Twenty-First Century*. 4th ed. Toronto: Oxford University Press, 2010.

Campbell, Heather, Malcom Tait, and Craig Watkins. "Is There Space for Better Planning in a Neoliberal World? Implications for Planning Practice and Theory." *Journal of Planning Education and Research* 34, no. 1 (2014): 45–59.

Carmon, Naomi. "Three Generations of Urban Renewal Policies: Analysis and Policy Implications." *Geoforum* 30 (1999): 45–58.

Carter, Tom. "Neighborhood Improvement: The Canadian Experience." In *Neighborhood Regeneration: An International Evaluation*, edited by Rachelle Alterman and Goran Cars, 9–22. London: Mansell Publishing, 1991.

Carter, Tom, and Chesya Polevychok. *Comprehensive Neighborhood Studies: Characterizing Decline*. Winnipeg: Institute of Urban Studies, 2003.

Cashmore, Ernest, and Eugene Mclaughlin. *Out of Order: Policing Black People*. London: Routledge, 1991.

Caulfield, Jon. *City Form and Everyday Life: Toronto's Gentrification and Critical Social Practice*. Toronto: University of Toronto Press, 1994.

Chambers, Robert. "The Origins and Practice of Participatory Rural Appraisal." *World Development* 22, no.7 (1994): 953–969.

———. "Participation in the Farmer-Owned Reserve Program: A Discrete Choice Model." *American Journal of Agricultural Economics* 65, no. 1 (1983): 120–124.

Chaskin, Robert J., and Mark L. Joseph. "Social Interaction in Mixed-Income Developments: Relational Expectations and Emerging Reality." *Journal of Urban Affairs* 33, no. 2 (2011): 209–237.

Chaskin, Robert J., Amy Khare, and Mark L. Joseph. "Participation, Deliberation, and Decision Making: The Dynamics of Inclusion and Exclusion in Mixed-Income Developments." *Urban Affairs Review* 48, no. 6 (2001): 863–906.

Chatterjee, Partha. *The Nation and Its Fragments: Colonial and Postcolonial Histories*. Princeton: Princeton University Press, 1993.

Cooke, Bill, and Uma Kothari. *Participation: The New Tyranny?* London: Zed, 2001.

Coulthard, Glen. *Red Skin, White Masks: Rejecting the Colonial Politics of Recognition*. Minneapolis: University of Minnesota Press, 2014.

Dávila, Arlene. *Barrio Dreams: Puerto Ricans, Latinos, and the Neoliberal City*. Berkeley: University of California Press, 2004.

Davis, Mike. *City of Quartz: Excavating the Future in Los Angeles*. New York: Vintage Books, 1990.

———. *Planet of the Slums*. New York: Verso, 2006.

Day, Iyko. *Alien Capital: Asian Racialization and the Logic of Settler Colonial Capitalism*. Durham, NC: Duke University Press, 2016.

Defilippis, James, and Jim Fraser. "Why Do We Want Mixed-Income Housing and Neighborhoods?" In *Critical Urban Studies: New Directions*, edited by Jonathan Davies and David Imbroscio, 135–148. Albany: State University of New York Press, 2010.

Dose, Jennifer, and Richard Klimoski. "The Diversity of Diversity: Work Values Effects on Formative Team Processes." *Human Resources Management* 9, no. 1 (1999): 83–108.

Egan, Brian. "Recognition Politics and Reconciliation Fantasies: Liberal Multiculturalism and the 'Indian Land Question.'" In *Home and Native Land: Unsettling Multiculturalism in Canada*, edited by May Chazan, Lisa Helps, Anna Stanley, and Sonali Thakkar, 123–141. Toronto: Between the Lines, 2001.

Fainstein, Susan. "Cities and Diversity: Should We Want It? Can We Plan for It? *Urban Affairs Review* 41, no. 1 (2005): 3–19.

———. *The Just City*. Ithaca: Cornell University Press, 2010.

Fanon, Frantz. *Black Skin, White Masks*. New York: Grove Press, 1967.

Filion, Pierre. "Core Redevelopment, Neighbourhood Revitalization and Municipal Government Motivation: Twenty Years of Urban Renewal in Quebec City." *Canadian Journal of Political Science* 2 (1987): 131–147.

———. "The Neighbourhood Improvement Plan: Montreal and Toronto: Contrasts Between a Participatory and a Centralized Approach to Urban Policy Making." *Urban History Review* 17 (1988): 16–28.

Fincher, Ruth, and Kurt Iveson. *Planning and Diversity in the City: Redistribution, Recognition, and Encounter*. New York: Palgrave Macmillian, 2008.

Flint, Colin, ed. *Spaces of Hate: Geographies of Discrimination and Intolerance in the U.S.* New York: Routledge, 2004.

Forester, John. *Critical Theory, Public Policy, and Planning Practice: Toward a Critical Pragmatism*. New York: State University of New York Press, 1993.

———. *Planning in the Face of Power*. Berkeley: University of California Press, 1989.

Foucault, Michel. "Discipline." *In Rethinking the Subject: An Anthology of Contemporary European Social Thought*, edited by James D. Faubion, 32–33. New York: Routledge, 1995.

Galabuzi, Grace-Edward. *Canada's Economic Apartheid: The Social Exclusion of Racialized Groups in The New Century*. Toronto: Canadian Scholars Press Inc, 2006.

Garb, Margaret. *City of American Dreams: A History of Homeownership and Housing Reform in Chicago, 1871–1919*. Chicago: University of Chicago Press, 2005.

Gilbert, Liette, Punam Khosla, and Feike De Jong. "Precaritization and Urban Growth in Mexico City." *Espacialidades, Revista de Temas Contemporáneos Sobre Lugares, Política y Cultura* 6, no. 2 (July–December 2016): 6–32.

Glass, Ruth. *London: Aspects of Change*. Centre for Urban Studies Report No. 3. Edited by the Centre for Urban Studies. London: University College London, 1964.

Goetz, Edward. *New Deal Ruins: Race, Economic Justice, and Public Housing Policy*. Ithaca, NY: Cornell University Press, 2013.

Goldberg, David Theo. *Racist Culture*. Malden, MA: Blackwell Publishers, 1993.

———. *The Threat of Race: Reflections on Racial Neoliberalism*. Malden, MA: Wiley Blackwell, 2009.

Goonewardena, Kanishka, and Stefan Kipfer. "Spaces of Difference: Reflections from Toronto on Multiculturalism, Bourgeois Urbanism and the Possibility of Radical Urban Politics." *International Journal of Urban and Regional Research* 29, no. 3 (2005): 670–678.

Gotham, Kevin Fox. "A City without Slums: Urban Renewal, Public Housing and Downtown Revitalization in Kansas City, Missouri." *American Journal of Economics and Sociology* 60, no. 1 (2001): 285–316.

———. "Urban Redevelopment, Past and Present." *Critical Perspectives on Urban Redevelopment* 6 (2001): 1–31.

Graham, Stephen. *Cities Under Siege: The New Military Urbanism.* London: Verso, 2010.

Grodach, Carl, and Renia Ehrenfeucht. *Urban Revitalization: Remaking Cities in a Changing World.* New York: Routledge, 2015.

Gutmann, Amy. *Multiculturalism: Examining the Politics of Recognition.* Princeton: Princeton University Press, 1994.

Hackworth, Jason. "The Durability of Roll-Out Neoliberalism under Center-Left Governance: The Case of Ontario's Social Housing Sector." *Studies in Political Economy* 81 (2008.): 7–26.

Hackworth, Jason, and Abigail Moriah. "Neoliberalism, Contingency, and Urban Policy: The Case of Social Housing in Ontario." *International Journal of Urban and Regional Research* 30, no. 3 (2006): 510–527.

Hackworth, Jason, and Neil Smith. "The Changing State of Gentrification." *Journal of Economic and Social Geography* 92, no. 4 (2002): 464–477.

Hall, Stuart. "Conclusion: The Multicultural Question." In *Un/Settled Multiculturalisms,* edited by Barnor Hesse, 209–241. London: Zed Books, 2000.

Harney, Stefano, and Fred Moten. *The Undercommons: Fugitive Planning and Black Study.* Wivenhoe, New York: Minor Compositions, 2013.

Harvey, David. *A Brief History of Neoliberalism.* New York: Oxford University Press, 2005.

———. *The Urbanization of Capital: Studies in the History of Theory of Capitalist Urbanization.* Baltimore: Johns Hopkins University Press, 1985.

Healey, Patsy. *Collaborative Planning: Shaping Places in Fragmented Societies.* Vancouver: University of British Columbia Press, 1997.

———. "The Communicative Turn in Planning Theory and Its Implications for Spatial Strategy Formation." *Environment and Planning B: Planning and Design* 23, no. 2 (1996): 217–234.

Hickey, Samuel, and Giles Mohan, eds. *Participation: From Tyranny to Transformation? Exploring New Approaches to Participation in Development.* London: Zed Books, 2004.

Horak, Martin, and Alexander Moore. "Policy Shift without Institutional Change: The Precarious Place of Neighborhood Revitalization in Toronto." In *Urban Neighborhoods in a New Era: Revitalization Politics in the Postindustrial City,* edited by Clarence N. Stone and Robert Stoker, 182–208. Chicago: University of Chicago Press, 2015.

Hulchanski, J. David. "What Factors Shape Canadian Housing Policy? The Intergovernmental Role in Canada's Housing System." In *Canada: The State of the*

Federation — Municipal, Federal, Provincial Relations in Canada 2004, edited by
    Robert Young and Christian Leuprecht, 221–245. Montreal: McGill-Queen's
    University Press, 2006.

Hulchanski, J. David, and Michael Shapcott, eds. *Finding Room: Policy Options for a
    Canadian Rental Housing Strategy*. Toronto: University of Toronto Press, 2004.

Innes, Judith. "Planning Theory's Emerging Paradigm: Communicative Action and
    Interactive Practice." *Journal of Planning Education and Research* 14, no. 3 (1995):
    183–189.

Israel, Emil, and Amnon Frenkel. "Social Justice and Spatial Inequality: Toward a
    Conceptual Framework." *Progress in Human Geography* 42, no. 5 (2018): 647–665.

Jacobs, Jane. *The Life and Death of Great American Cities*. New York: Vintage Books,
    1992 (1961).

Jacobs, Jane M. *Edge of Empire: Postcolonialism and the City*. New York: Routledge, 1996.

James, Carl. "Up to No Good": Black on the Streets and Encountering Police. In
    Racism and Social Inequality in Canada, edited by Vic Satzewich, 157–178. Toronto:
    Thompson Books, 1998.

James, Ryan K. "'Slum Clearance' to 'Revitalisation': Planning, Expertise and Moral
    Regulation in Toronto's Regent Park." *Planning Perspectives* 25, no. 1 (2010): 69–86.

Jessop, Bob. "Neoliberalism, and Urban Governance: A State-Theoretical
    Perspective." *Antipode* 34, no. 3 (2002): 452–472,

Johnson, Laura C., and Robert E. Johnson. *Regent Park Redux: Reinventing Public
    Housing in Canada*. London: Routledge, 2017.

Joseph, Mark L., and Robert J. Chaskin. "Mixed-Income Developments and Low
    Rates of Return: Insights from Relocated Public Housing Residents in Chicago."
    Housing Policy Debate 22, no. 3 (2012): 377–406.

Joseph, Mark L., Robert J. Chaskin, and Henry S. Webber. "The Theoretical Basis for
    Addressing Poverty through Mixed-Income Development." *Urban Affairs Review*
    42, no. 3 (2007): 369–409.

Kapoor, Ilan. "Participatory Development, Complicity and Desire." *Third World
    Quarterly* 26, no. 8 (2005): 1203–1220.

Keil, Roger. "'Common–Sense' Neoliberalism: Progressive Conservative Urbanism
    in Toronto, Canada." *Antipode* 34, no. 3 (2002): 578–601.

Keil, Roger, and Stefan Kipfer. "Toronto Inc? Planning the Competitive City in the
    New Toronto." *Antipode* 34, no. 2 (2002): 227–264.

Khare, Amy, Mark L. Joseph, and Robert J. Chaskin. "The Enduring Signficance of
    Race in Mixed-Income Developments." *Urban Affairs Review* 51, no. 4 (2015):
    474–503.

Khenti, Akwatu. "The Canadian War on Drugs: Structural Violence and Unequal
    Treatment of Black Canadians." *International Journal of Drug Policy* 25, no. 2 (2014):
    190–195.

Kipfer, Stefan, and Jason Petrunia. "Recolonization and Public Housing: A Toronto
    Case Study." *Studies in Political Economy* 83 (2009): 111–139.

Kymlicka, Will. *Multicultural Citizenship: A Liberal Theory of Minority Rights*. Oxford:
    Oxford University Press, 1996.

————. "The Rise and Fall of Multiculturalism? New Debates on Inclusion and Accommodation in Diverse Societies." *International Social Science Journal* 61, no. 199 (2010): 97–112.

————. "The Theory and Practice of Canadian Multiculturalism." Lectures hosted by the Humanities and Social Science Federation of Canada, 1988.

Lacher, Hannes. "Embedded Liberalism, Disembedded Markets: Reconceptualising the Pax Americana." *New Political Economy* 4 (1999): 343–360.

Lees, Loretta. "Gentrification and Social Mixing: Towards An Inclusive Urban Renaissance?" *Urban Studies* 45, no. 12 (2008): 2449–2470.

Lees, Loretta, Tom Slater, and Elvin Wyly. *Gentrification*. New York: Routledge, 2008.

Lefebvre, Henri. *The Production of Space*, translated By Donald Nicholson-Smith. Malden, MA: Wiley Blackwell, 1992.

Lewis, Oscar. *Five Families: Mexican Case Studies in the Culture of Poverty*. New York: Basic Books, 1959.

————. *La Vida: A Puerto Rican Family in the Culture of Poverty—San Juan and New York*. New York: Vintage, 1966.

Ley, David. "Inner City Revitalization in Canada: A Vancouver Case Study." *Canadian Geographer* 25 (1981): 124–148.

————. "Myths and Meanings of Immigration and the Metropolis." *Canadian Geographer* 43 (1999): 2–19.

Lipsitz, George. "Learning from New Orleans: The Social Warrant of Hostile Privatism and Competitive Consumer Citizenship." *Cultural Anthropology* 21, no. 3 (2006): 451–468.

Loh, Carolyn G., and Rose Kim. "Are We Planning for Equity?" *Journal of the American Planning Association* 87, no. 2 (2021): 181–196.

MacDonald, David. "Aboriginal Peoples and Multicultural Reform in Canada: Prospects for a New Binational Society." *Canadian Journal of Sociology* 38, no.1 (2014): 65–86.

Mackey, Eva. *The House of Difference: Cultural Politics and National Identity in Canada*. Toronto: University of Toronto Press, 2002.

Madden, David J., and Peter Marcuse. *In Defense of Housing: The Politics of Crisis*. London: Verso, 2016.

Manaugh, Kevin, Madhav Badami, and Ahmed El-Geneidy. "Integrating Social Equity into Urban Transportation Planning: A Critical Evaluation of Equity Objectives and Measures in Transportation Plans in North America." *Transport Policy* 37 (January 2015): 167–176.

Marshall, Tomas Humphrey. *Citizenship and Social Class, and Other Essays*. London: Cambridge University Press, 1950.

Maynard, Robyn. *Policing Black Lives: State Violence in Canada from Slavery to the Present*. Blackpoint, NS: Fernwood Publishing, 2017.

Mcclusky, Martha. "Efficiency and Social Citizenship: Challenging the Neoliberal Attack on the Welfare State." *Indiana Law Journal* 78 (2002): 799–872.

McCready, A. L. "Redressing Redress: The Neoliberal Appropriation of Redress in the Anti-Native Backlash at Caledonia." *English Studies in Canada* 35, no. 1 (2009): 162–190.

McKittrick, Katherine. *Demonic Grounds: Black Women and the Cartographies of Struggle*. Minneapolis: University of Minnesota Press, 2006.

Meerow, Sara, Pani Pajouhesh, and Thaddeus Miller. "Social Equity in Urban Resilience Planning." *Local Environment* 24, no. 9 (2019): 793–808.

Melamed, Jodi. "The Spirit of Neoliberalism: From Racial Liberalism to Neoliberal Multiculturalism." *Social Text* 89, vol. 24, no. 4 (2006): 1–24.

Metzger, John T. "The Theory and Practice of Equity Planning: An Annotated Bibliography." *Journal of Planning Literature* 11, no. 1 (1996): 112–126.

Michaels, Walter Benn. *The Trouble with Diversity: How We Learned to Love Identity and Ignore Inequality*. New York: Metropolitan Books, 2006.

Mills, Charles. *Black Rights/White Wrongs: The Critique of Racial Liberalism*. New York: Oxford University Press, 2017.

Miraftab, Faranak. "Public Private Partnerships: The Trojan Horse of Neoliberal Development." *Journal of Planning Education and Research* 24, no. 1 (2004): 89–101.

Modood, Tariq. *Multiculturalism: A Civic Idea*. Cambridge: Polity Press, 2007.

Moore Aaron, and Jordana Wright. "Toronto's Market-Oriented Subsidised Housing PPPs: A Risk Worth the Reward?" *Cities* 69 (2017): 64–72.

Nelson, Jennifer. "The Space of Africville: Creating, Regulating, and Remembering the Urban Slum." In *Race, Space, and the Law: Unsettling a White Settler Society*, edited by Sherene Razack, 211–232. Toronto: Between The Lines, 2002.

Newman, Oscar. *Defensible Space: Crime Prevention through Urban Design*. New York: Macmillan, 1972.

Oxford English Dictionary and Thesaurus. Oxford English Dictionary 2nd Edition, 2007.

Oxford English Dictionary. Oxford University Press, 2020.

Pateman, Carole. *Participation and Democratic Theory*. London: Cambridge University Press, 1975.

Peck, Jaimie, Nik Theodore, and Neil Brenner. "Variegated Neoliberalization: Geographies, Modalities, Pathways." *Antipode* 10, no. 2 (2009): 182–222.

Peck, Jaimie, and Adam Tickell. "Neoliberalizing Space." *Antipode* 34, no. 3 (2002): 380–404.

Pickett, Stanley H. "An Appraisal of the Urban Renewal Programme in Canada." *University of Toronto Law Journal* 18, no. 3 (1968): 233–247.

Pitter, Jay. "Reconsidering Revitalization: The Case of Regent Park. In Conversation with Sandra Costain." In *Subdivided: City Building in an Age of Hyper-Diversity*, edited by Jay Pitter and John Lorinc, 176–184. Toronto: Coach House Books, 2016.

Povenelli, Elizabeth. *The Cunning of Recognition: Indigenous Alterities and the Making of Australian Multiculturalism*. Durham, NC: Duke University Press, 2002.

Purcell, Mark. "Resisting Neoliberalization: Communicative Planning or Counter-Hegemonic Movements?" *Planning Theory* 8, no. 2 (2009): 140–165.

Purdy, Sean. "Building Homes, Building Citizens: Housing Reform and Nation Formation in Canada, 1900-1920." *Canadian Historical Review* 79, no. 2 (1998): 492–523.

———. "'Ripped Off' by the System: Housing Policy, Poverty, and Territorial Stigmatization in Regent Park Housing Project, 1951-1991." *Labour/Le Travail* 52 (2003): 45–108.

—————. "Scaffolding Citizenship: Housing Reform and Nation Formation in Canada, 1900–1950." In *Contesting Canadian Citizenship*, edited by Robert Adamoski, Dorothy Chunn, and Robert Menzies, 129–154. Toronto: Broadview Press, 2013.

Razack, Sherene, ed. *Race, Space, and the Law: Unmapping a White Settler Society*. Toronto: Between The Lines, 2002.

Razack, Sherene, Malinda Smith, and Sunera Thobani. *States of Race: Critical Race Feminism for the 21st Century*. Toronto: Between The Lines, 2010.

Roberts, Dorothy E. *Crime, Race, and Reproduction*. Faculty Scholarship at University of Pennsylvania Law 1383 (1993).

Roberts, Peter, and Hugh Sykes. *Urban Regeneration: A Handbook*. London: SAGE Publications, 2000.

Robinson, Matthew B. The Theoretical Development of CPTED: 25 Years of Responses to C. Ray Jeffery. *Advances in Criminological Theory* 8 (1996): 427–462.

Rosa, Vanessa. "Interrogating Multiculturalism and Urban Revitalization: The Diversity of Diversity in Toronto's Regent Park." *Journal of Critical Race Inquiry* 6, no. 1 (2019): 32–61.

—————. "Social Citizenship and Urban Revitalization in Canada." *Canadian Journal of Urban Research* 27, no. 2 (2018): 25–36.

Rose, Albert. *Canadian Housing Policies, 1935–1980*. Toronto: Butterworths, 1980.

—————. *Governing Metropolitan Toronto: A Social and Political Analysis, 1953–1971*. Berkeley: University of California Press, 1972.

—————. *Regent Park: A Study in Slum Clearance*. Toronto: University of Toronto Press, 1958.

Rosenbaum, Dennis. "The Theory and Research Behind Neighborhood Watch: Is It a Sound Fear and Crime Reduction Strategy?" *Crime and Delinquency* 33, no. 1 (1987): 103–134.

Rosenthal, Donald B., ed. "Urban Revitalization." *Urban Affairs Annual Reviews* 18. London: SAGE Publications, 1980.

Rowe, Daniel J., and James R. Dunn. "Tenure and Mix in Toronto: Resident Attitudes and Experience in the Regent Park Community." *Housing Studies* 30, no. 8 (2016): 1257–1280.

Saberi, Parastou. "Toronto and the 'Paris Problem': Community Policing in 'Immigrant Neighbourhoods.'" *Race and Class* 59, no. 2 (2017): 49–69.

Sandercock, Leoni. *Towards Cosmopolis: Planning for Multicultural Cities*. New York: John Wiley, 1998.

Sanders, Heywood T. "Urban Renewal and the Revitalized City: A Consideration of Recent History." In *Urban Revitalization*, edited by Donald Rosenthal, 103–126. *Urban Affairs Annual Reviews* 18. London: SAGE Publications, 1980.

Sassen, Saskia. *The Global City: New York, London, and Tokyo*. Princeton: Princeton University Press, 1991.

—————. *Globalization and Its Discontents: Essays on the New Mobility of People and Money*. New York: New Press, 1998.

Schwartz, Alex. *Housing Policy in the United States*. New York: Routledge, 2015.

Schweitzer, John, June Woo Kim, and Juliette R. Mackin. "The Impact of the Built Environment on Crime and Fear of Crime in Urban Neighborhoods." *Journal of Technology* 6, no. 3 (1999): 59–73.

Sewell, John. *Houses and Homes: Housing For Canadians*. Toronto: James Lorimer and Company, 1994.

Sharma, Nandita. *Home Economics: Nationalism and the Making of 'Migrant Workers' in Canada*. Toronto: University of Toronto Press, 2006.

Shaw, Kate. "Gentrification: What Is It, Why It Is, and What Can Be Done About It." *Geography Compass* 2, no. 5 (2008): 1–32.

Slater, Tom. "Gentrification in Canada's Cities: From Social Mix to Social Tectonics?" In *Gentrification in a Global Context: The New Urban Colonialism*, edited by Rowland Atkinson and Gary Bridge, 39–56. New York: Routledge, 2005.

Smelser, Neil J., and Jeffrey Alexander. *Diversity and Its Discontents: Cultural Conflict and Common Ground in Contemporary American Society*. Princeton: Princeton University Press, 1999.

Smith, Neil. "Gentrification and Uneven Development." *Economic Geography* 58, (1982): 139–155.

———. "New Globalism, New Urbanism: Gentrification as a Global Urban Strategy." *Antipode* 34, no. 3 (2002): 427–450.

———. *The New Urban Frontier: Gentrification and the Revanchist City*. New York: Routledge, 1996.

———. "Toward a Theory of Gentrification: A Back to the City Movement by Capital, Not People." *Journal of the American Planning Association* 45, no. 4 (1979): 538–548.

Smith, Peter J., and Peter W. Moore. "Cities as a Social Responsibility: Planning and Urban Form." In *The Changing Geography of Canadian Cities*, edited by Larry Bourne and David Ley, 343–366. Montreal: Mcgill-Queen's University Press, 1993.

Soja, Edward. *Thirdspace: Journeys to Los Angeles and Other Real and Imagined Places*. Malden, MA: Blackwell, 1996.

Statistics Canada. 2006 Census. Ottawa: Statistics Canada, 2006.

Stein, Samuel. *Capital City: Gentrification and the Real Estate State*. London: Verso, 2019.

Tator, Carol, and Frances Henry. *Racial Profiling: Challenging the Myth of "A Few Bad Apples."* Toronto: University of Toronto Press, 2006.

Taylor, Charles. *Multiculturalism and the Politics of Recognition*. Princeton: Princeton University Press, 1994.

Taylor, Harry. "Insights into Participation from Critical Management and Labour Process Perspectives." In *Participation: The New Tyranny?*, edited by Bill Cooke and Uma Kothari, 122–152. London: Zed, 2001.

Teelucksingh, Cheryl, ed. *Claiming Space: Racialization in Canadian Cities*. Waterloo, ON: Wilfred Laurier Press, 2006.

Thobani, Sunera. *Exalted Subjects: Studies in the Making of Race and Nation in Canada*. Toronto: University of Toronto Press, 2007.

Toews, Owen. *Stolen City: Racial Capitalism and the Making of Winnipeg*. Winnipeg: ARP Books, 2018.

Vale, Lawrence J., and Shomon Shamsuddin. "All Mixed Up: Making Sense of Mixed-Income Housing Developments." *Journal of the American Planning Association* 83, no. 1 (2017): 56–67.

Valverde, Mariana. "The Ethic of Diversity: Local Law and the Negotiation of Urban Norms." *Law and Social Inquiry* 33, no. 4 (2008): 895–923.

———. *Everyday Law on the Street: Governance in an Age of Diversity*. Chicago: University of Chicago Press, 2012.

———. "A Tale of Two—or Three—Cities: Gentrification and Community Consultations." In *Subdivided: City Building in an Age of Hyper-Diversity*, edited by Jay Pitter and John Lorinc, 199–207. Toronto: Coach House Books, 2016.

Vertovec, Steven. "Super-Diversity and its Implications." *Ethnic and Racial Studies* 30, no. 6 (2007): 1024–1054.

Wagner, Fritz W., Timothy E. Joder, and Anthony J. Mumphrey. *Urban Revitalization: Policies and Programs*. London: SAGE Publications, 1995.

Walks, Alan. "Global City, Global Housing Bubble? Toronto's Housing Bubble and Its Discontents." In *Critical Dialogues of Urban Governance, Development and Activism: London and Toronto*, edited by Susannah Bunce, Nicola Livingstone, Loren March, Susan Moore, and Alan Walks, 130–144. London: UCL Press, 2020.

Westin, Martin. "The Framing of Power in Communicative Planning Theory: Analysing the Work of John Forester, Patsy Healey and Judith Innes." *Planning Theory* 21, no. 2 (2022): 132–154.

Wharton, Jonathan L. "Gentrification as the New Colonialism." *Forum on Public Policy: A Journal of the Oxford Round Table*, Summer 2008. Gale Academic OneFile, https://link.gale.com/apps/doc/A218606468/AONE?u=mlin_oweb&sid =googleScholar&xid=b61ad89e.

Wilson, David. "Toward a Contingent Urban Neoliberalism." *Urban Geography* 25 (2004): 771–783.

Wilson, James. *Urban Renewal: The Record and the Controversy*. Cambridge, MA: MIT Press, 1966.

Woods, Clyde. *Development Arrested: The Blues and Plantation Power in the Mississippi Delta*. London: Verso, 1998.

Young, Alford. *The Minds of Marginalized Black Men: Making Sense of Mobility, Opportunity and Future Life Chances*. Princeton: Princeton University Press, 2004.

Yuval-Davis, Nira. *Gender and Nation*. London: SAGE Publications, 1997.

Zapparoli, David. *Regent Park: The Public Experiment in Housing*. Toronto: Hushion House Publishing, 1999.

Unpublished Theses, Dissertations, and Papers

Fennell, Catherine K. "The Last Project Standing: Building an Ethics for the City without Public Housing." PhD diss. Chicago: University of Chicago, 2009.

Spalding, Ashley E. "Race, Class, and Real Estate: Neoliberal Policies in a Mixed-Income Neighborhood." PhD diss. Tampa: University of South Florida, 2008.

Index

Canadian national identity, 1, 5, 55–58; construction of, 4, 17, 80, 107; contestation of, 4; core values of, 94, 103, 125n31; cultural differences and, 8, 75; diversity and, 8; immigrants and, 75; multiculturalism and, 8, 10, 62, 64; normative construction of, 70–71; promotion of, 16; reproduction of, 4; symbols of, 6; teaching of, 15–16; values and, 75

Canadianness, 55–56, 105, 106; community security practices and, 57–58; construction of, 80; core values of, 64; cultural diversity and, 63; teaching how to be Canadian, 77–78, 103. *See also* Canadian national identity

"Canadian way," 105–6

Cappe, Lorne, 62

Carby, Jermaine, 58

Caribbean communities, 25, 32

Chambers, Robert, 79

Chandra, 41–43, 46, 66, 70–71, 76, 96–97, 101, 103–4, 112, 125n34

chapter map, 14–16

Chaskin, Robert J., 43, 44, 123n28

Chicago School of Sociology, 9

children: lack of resources for, 67; participation and, 105–6; safety of, 68, 73. *See also* youth outreach

Chinatown, Vancouver, British Columbia, 25

Chinese, 30

Chinese Head Tax, 1, 115n3

Chippewa people, 19

citizenship, 4, 5

CivicAction, 25

civic engagement, 77–79, 102–3. *See also* engagement

civics, 77–78

class, 1, 3, 4, 93, 106–7; behavior and, 63–64; crime and, 65–66; difference between, 63; disparity of, 38–39, 54, 63–64, 65–66, 93; diversity and, 64; hierarchy of, 1, 4; and inferiority, 106–7; negotiating, 65–66; power relations and, 94–95; presupposition of inferiority and, 106–7; privilege, 73; race and, 54; racialization and, 54; safety and, 73; segregation by, 106–7; stereotypes of, 93; stigmatization and, 93; subjugation reproduced via neoliberal multiculturalism, 3

classism, 43, 48

collaboration, 104

collaborative planning, 79–80, 81–85

Colour of Poverty, 112

communications, 104; community consultations and, 88–90, 98–101; shortcomings of, 93–96; TCHC and, 90–91

communicative planning, 79–80

communities, homogenization of, 80

communities of color, 2; hyperpolicing and, 60–61. *See also specific groups*

community, 62, 64, 106; conceptions of, 64, 71, 76, 80; framing of concept, 80; as untapped resource, 64, 68–71

community activism, lack of, 88

community activities, 13, 84, 105–6

community animators, 82, 85, 98–99

community building, 56

community consultations, 2–5, 10, 13, 64, 82–83, 86–97, 104, 128n69; aspects left out of, 104; communication and, 88–90, 98–101; contesting, 80, 97–102; diversity and, 107–8; limitations of, 96–97; mandated, 3; participation in, 77–80; power dynamics of, 97–98; shift in effectiveness of, 90–91

community engagement, 77–103

community formations, crime and, 64, 66–68

community infrastructure, strengthening of, 82

community-led transformation, 98, 112

community meetings, 13. *See also* community consultations

community members, "empowering," 79

deregulation, housing policy and, 26–27

design: codes of behavior and, 60–61; material design of spaces, 60–61, 75, 125n28; outdated design of Regent Park, 22; safety and, 70–71; security and, 70–71; spatial design, 60–61; urban design, 15. *See also* Crime Prevention through Environmental Design (CPTED)

developers: private, 4; tenant involvement in selection of, 85

development, 78; neoliberalism and, 10–11

development teams, 80

Diana, 77, 89, 95–96, 103

difference, 3–4, 8; communities and, 80; cultural framing of, 8; exclusion and, 77–78; multiculturalism and, 9; naturalization of, 16; positioning and, 77–78; reinscription of, 9. *See also specific kinds of difference*

disadvantaged groups, engagement of, 80

discipline, 3; as technology, 3; as type of power, 3

disparity, 3; diversity and, 16

displacement, 117n61

diversity, 2–5, 9–10, 14, 17, 58, 77–78, 106, 109; of building types, 9; Canadian national identity and, 8; celebrations of, 8; class disparity and, 64; community consultations and, 107–8; concept of, 38–39; constructed as celebration of culture, 3; construction of, 107; constructions of, 112; as contested concept, 39; critical planning and, 9–10; of culture, 14, 37–38, 43, 49–52 (see cultural diversity); definitions of, 39; discourse of, 53–54; disparity and, 16; of diversities, 14, 43, 52–53, 54, 122n7; flexibility of the term, 10; governance and, 14; hierarchy of, 104; inclusion and, 10; of income, 14, 37–38, 43, 43–49, 52–53, 63; *mix* and, 54;

multiculturalism and, 38, 47; participation and, 107–8; in planning discourses, 38–54; of population, 45; relationship between types of, 51–52; of residents, 9; revitalization and, 14–15, 37–54; rhetoric of, 37–54; social vs. physical, 10; surveillance and, 14–15, 63; of tenure, 45–46; as tool of neoliberal multiculturalism, 63; of use, 14, 37–38, 39–43, 52, 53; used to signal income, 46; use of the term, 37, 44–46; as value, 4

diversity, equity, and inclusion (DEI), pluralism and, 9–10

diversity of diversities, 14, 43, 52–53, 54, 122n7

diversity of income, 14, 37–38, 43–49, 52–53, 63–64

diversity of use, 14, 37–38, 39–43, 52, 53

"diversity speak," 53, 109

Dixon Hall, 42

Dominion Housing Act, 20

Don Mount Court, 28

Don Valley Parkway, 20

Dose, Jennifer, 122n7

Downsview Airport, 24

Dunn, James R., 48

Earls, Felton, 60

East African communities, 32

economic development, 84

economic diversity, 3

economic inequality, 26

economic reinvestment, 14

Egan, Brian, 105

embodiment, 107

empowerment, 79, 80, 84; community voice and, 98; engagement and, 86–87

encounters, negotiated and normalized, 71–75

engagement, 78, 79–80, 81–85; democracy and, 85–86; of disadvantaged groups, 80; empowerment and, 86–87; goals of engagement process, 82; lack of substantive, 91; omissions from engagement process, 87; participation and, 103; planning process and, 81–85; youth and, 84

English culture and language, 6–7, 32

"entrepreneurial" approach, 4

environmental design. See Crime Prevention through Environmental Design (CPTED)

environmental scan, 81–82

equality, 9. See also inequality

equity, 9–10

essentialism, preventing, 80

ethnic differences, 8, 9

ethnic integration, local governments and, 9

ethnic studies, 9

"ethnocultural" groups, 6–7

Euro-Canadian neighborhoods, 25

Europe, models from, 44

Eva, 66–67, 68, 71, 73, 74, 93–94, 103

events, 13

exclusion, 1, 3, 14, 56, 103, 106, 108–9; alternatives to, 105–6; difference and, 77–78; Indigenous peoples and, 9, 17; by language and culture, 82

"eyes on the street," 55–57, 59, 61–62, 66, 71, 75, 76, 107, 125n32

Fainstein, Susan, 10

federal government, 5, 6–7; changes in housing policy in 1990s, 26–27; cultural differences and, 7–8, 9; housing policy and, 14, 18; provincial governments and, 23, 27–28; public infrastructure improvements and, 44; social housing and, 27

Federal Urban Renewal Program, 20

feminist approaches, 8

fieldwork, 13

financial framework, 4, 103, 104

food insecurity, 35

Ford, Doug, 110

Ford, Rob, 34

Foucault, Michel, 3

Francophones, 6–7, 82

free market, 10, 11

French culture and language, 6–7, 82

gentrification, 25–26, 31, 43, 108–9, 117n59, 117n61; capitalism and, 11–12; class and, 11–12; definitions of, 11–12; neoliberalism and, 11; as new colonialism, 12–13; of Regent Park, 41; revitalization and, 11, 53, 54; "sporadic," 26; state-managed, 26

Glass, Ruth, 11

Globe and Mail, 22

governance: diversity and, 14; laissez-faire, 11; urban, 2, 11

government, 5. See also federal government; local governments; provincial governments

governmentality, strategies of, 75

Graham, Stephen, 56

Greg, 65, 71, 87, 100–101, 125n32

guaranteed basic income, 110, 111

Gutmann, Amy, 6

Hackworth, Jason, 11

Hall, Stuart, 6

Hamilton, Ontario, 58

hardship, Indigenous peoples and, 17

Harney, Stefano, 111

Harper, Stephen, 7, 8

Harris government, 27

Harvey, David, 10

Haudenosaunee people, 19

Heritage Interpretation Plan, 83, 84, 102

heterogeneity, 80

hierarchy: class hierarchy, 1, 4; of diversity, 104; race hierarchy, 4; reinscription of, 9; reproduction of, 17

historical preservation, 84

home: concept of, 17; construction of, 17; modernist ideas of, 17

homeland, construction of, 17

homeownership: homeownership programs, 21; public housing as stepping stone to, 26

home prices, 34
homes, housing and, 5
homogenization, 80
Horak, Martin, 28, 36
houselessness, 109
housing, 10–11; citizenship and, 5; commodification of, 28; construction of, 17, 108; deregulation of, 26; growing housing costs, 26; homes and, 5; inadequate, 109; indigenous housing, 27; market-rate, 46–47; mixed-income housing, 43; redevelopment and, 26–27
housing justice, 109–12
housing policy, 5, 18–35; in Canada, 19–20; capitalism and, 28; changes in 1990s, 26, 44; deregulation and, 26–27; federal government and, 18; history of, 14; local governments and, 18; neoliberalism and, 18, 27–28; neoliberal restructuring of, 27–28; provincial governments and, 18; state intervention in, 28; in United States, 19–20
housing projects: segregation and, 37–38; in Toronto, Ontario, 17
housing shortages, 26, 44
housing stock, deteriorating, 87–88
housing waitlists, 109
Hulchanski, David, 5
hyperpolicing, 17, 60–61

ideal communities, existence of, 68
"ideal" neighborhood, 102–3
immigrants, 24–25, 30, 56, 62, 77–78, 103; Canadian identity and, 75; integration of, 7, 17; in the media, 75; policing and, 75
immigrant status, 4
immigration policy, 25
inclusion, 3–4, 9–10, 14, 16–17, 38, 43, 84, 94, 103, 108–9, 125n31; diversity and, 10; participatory planning and, 80; projection of, 16; recognition and, 106; as technology of governance, 106

income, diversity of, 14, 37–38, 43–49, 52–53, 63
income inequality, 26
income levels, crime and, 66, 125n34
Income Security Advocacy Centre, 112
indigenous housing, 27
Indigenous peoples, 2, 35, 82; attempted extermination of, 12; brutal treatment of, 1; exclusion and, 17; exclusion of, 9; hardship and, 17; hyperpolicing and, 17; indigenous housing, 27; multiculturalism and, 17; residential schooling an, 1; segregation and, 17; violence and, 17
inequality, 9, 26, 49, 108–9; addressing, 5; class, 3; democracy and, 3; economic inequality, 26; ethnoracial, 3; growing, 35; income inequality, 26; naturalization of, 16; neoliberal, 17; racial inequality, 26; (re)production of, 3, 16; structural, 4–5, 8; structural inequality, 53; urban, 10
integration, 9, 10, 37–38, 47, 51, 54, 64, 105–6, 125n31; of immigrants, 7, 17; local governments and, 9; logic of, 66; multiculturalism and, 8; neoliberal multiculturalism and, 106–7; promotion of, 2; superficial, 8
Intercolonial railway, 1
interventions, 106–9; abolitionist planning, 111; federal funding for social and public housing, 111; guaranteed basic income, 110, 111; national housing guarantee, 110, 111; reparations, 111
interview, 68
investment, 4, 11, 120n78. See also reinvestment
Ishaq, Zunera, 7
isolation, 62–63, 67; alternatives to, 105–6; crime and, 65–66; violence and, 65–66

Jacobs, Jane, 9, 56–57, 63
James, Ryan, 48
Jewish peoples, persecution of, 8
Johnson, Laura, 61
Johnson, Robert, 61
Joseph, Mark L., 43, 44, 123n28

Kaydeen, 101–2
Keynesianism, 10, 18
Khare, Amy, 123n28
Kipfer, Stefan, 24, 43, 52
Kiwubeyi, Albert, 72
Klimoski, Richard, 122n7
Kothari, Uma, 80
Kymlicka, Will, 7

labor: labor shortages, 25; management of, 12
laissez-faire governance, 11
Lake Ontario, 19
laneways, 92
language differences, 82–83. *See also specific languages*
Latin American communities, 25
Latino men, racial profiling of, 58
Laurendeau-Dunton Commission, *Multiculturalism within a Bilingual Framework*, 6–7
Lawrence-Allen, 120n78
Lawrence-Allen Revitalization Plan, 32–34, 61–62, 120n78; four themes of, 34
Lawrence Heights, 10, 12, 18, 27, 76, 105; 1940–1980, 23–24; already thriving and vibrant, 113; Canadian citizens at, 77–78; community consultations in, 86–97; consultation process and, 78, 83–85; crime in, 62–63, 65–66, 67; engagement process in, 83–85; historical preservation of, 84; histories of revitalization in, 14; history of, 23–24; isolation of, 62–63; as "The Jungle," 32; lack of history of community activism in, 88; lack of resource in, 67–68; Lawrence Manor

and, 13, 91–93, 95, 105; media coverage of planning process, 84; nicknamed the "jungle," 69, 70; planning documents from, 13; planning process in, 81–85; policing of, 68–69; popular media representations of, 32; population measurement, 120n79; profiling and stigmatization of, 69–70; public-private partnerships and, 29; racialization and, 25; racial spatial segregation in, 24–26; racial stigmatization of, 62; revitalization and, 26–34, 103, 108–9, 125–26n40; revitalization of, 26–27; secondary plan, 61–62; security state and, 14–15; shift in attitudes in, 85; Toronto, Ontario, 1
Lawrence Heights Inter-Organizational Alliance (LHION), 13
Lawrence Manor, 13, 91–93, 95, 105
Le Corbusier, 21
Leimonis, Vivi, 33
Leroy, 44
Lewis, Oscar, 123–24n55
liberal, definition of, 7
liberalism, normalized surveillance and, 75–76
liberal rights discourses, 18, 110
lighting, 72–73, 74
livability, 33–34, 62
local communities, empowerment of, 80
local governments, 5; ethnic integration and, 9; housing policy and, 14, 18
local police division 51, 72
local voice, 80
Loku, Andrew, 58
low-income residents, 3, 9, 30, 103; policing of, 63, 64; powerlessness of, 94–95; stigmatization of, 63–64; surveillance of, 63

Macdonald, John A., 1
Mackey, Eva, 9
Madden, David, 18

Neighborhood Improvement Program, 26
Neighborhood Watch, 59
neighborhood watch programs, 56–57
neoliberalism, 1–2, 10–11, 14, 17,
26–34, 75, 91–92, 111; definitions of,
10–11; entanglement of, 3–4; financial
framework and, 4; gentrification and,
11; housing policy and, 18; multiculturalism and, 3–4, 10, 12–13;
perspectives on, 11; poverty and,
48–49; "procedural participation" and,
15–16; redevelopment and, 5;
revitalization and, 18, 26–34, 26, 30,
38, 103; urban, 11; urban development and, 10–11; urban governance
and, 11
neoliberal multiculturalism, 1, 3, 112;
diversity as tool of, 63; integration
and, 106–7; normalized surveillance
and, 64; operationalization of, 107–8;
re-entrenchment of, 16; revitalization
and, 17; safety as tool of, 63; social
regulation and, 108–9
neoliberal surveillance, 55–75, 76
neoliberal urbanism, 34
neoliberal urban revitalization frameworks, introduced in late 1990s, 29
Neptune, 67–68, 85, 125–26n40
"newcomers," 77–78
newcomer status, 4
Newman, Oscar, 57
New York City, New York: crime rates
in, 57; New York City Housing
Authority, 28
New York State, 19
New York Times, 16–17, 39
Niagara Falls, 19
Nick, 60, 62–63, 88, 125n28
nonwhite residents, 3, 9, 56, 103, 109.
See also communities of color;
minorities; specific groups
normalized surveillance: liberalism and,
75–76; neoliberal multiculturalism
and, 64
North York, 23, 93, 105

North York Community Council,
93, 105

obsolescence, 28
One Cole Condominiums, 40
Ontario. See Province of Ontario
Ontario Coalition Against Poverty
(OCAP), 25, 112
Ontario Housing Corporation, 22
Ontario Planning act, 81
Oromo, 32

Pacific railway, 1
Pam McConnell Aquatic Center
(formerly Regent Park Aquatic
Center), 39–40, 43
"Paris Problem," 75
participation, 16, 102–3, 105–6, 112–13,
128n76; in community consultations,
77–78, 79–80; construction of, 107; in
consultation process, 15–16, 103–4;
democracy and, 79, 80, 85–86;
discourse of, 15–16; diversity and,
107–8; engagement and, 103;
frustrations of, 101–2; limitations on,
3; multiculturalism and, 80; in
planning process, 77–78, 79–80;
political, 17; procedural, 15–16,
85–97, 103; project of, 79–80;
revitalization and, 103; in surveillance, 76; surveillance and, 107. See
also participatory planning
participatory models, critiques of,
79–80
participatory planning, 79–80; essentialism and, 80; inclusion and, 80;
revitalization and, 80
"participatory reflection and action"
(PRA), 79, 80
Pearson Airport, 8
Peters, Ralph, 56
Petrunia, Jason, 24, 43, 52
physical diversity, 10
Pitter, Jay, 109
"place-making," 33, 62

revitalization, 2–5, 19–20, 66, 73, 108–9, 126n41; campaign to stop, 92–93; community efforts for, 87–88; consultation process and, 81–85; crime and, 69–70; criminalization and, 70–71; critique of, 104; cultural diversity and, 14; definitions of, 84, 112–13; diversity and, 14–15, 37–54; framing of, 16; funding of, 47–48; gentrification and, 11, 25–26, 53, 54; as "go-to planning approach, 36; history of, 87, 88, 109; holistic approach, 31; imposition of, 87, 88; Lawrence Heights and, 14, 26–34, 103, 108–9, 125–26n40; logic of, 26; media coverage of, 84; merits of, 52; neoliberalism and, 17–18, 26–34, 38, 103; neoliberal multiculturalism and, 17; opportunities made available through, 106, 112–13; participation and, 80, 103; participatory planning and, 80; place-based strategies, 26; political economy of, 10–13; private investment and, 30; procedural participation and, 85–97; public housing and, 1–2, 5; racial logics and, 106–7; Regent Park and, 14, 26–34, 37–54, 108–9; Regent Park as model for, 16–17; reproduction of social inequality and, 16; revitalization frameworks, 36, 83; revitalization process, 3–4; security and, 57–58; settler colonial capitalism and, 12–13; sociospatial history of, 109; surveillance and, 57–58, 71, 73–74, 76; United States and, 27; urban, 2; as urban governance tool, 12–13; violence and, 69–70; vs. welfare state policies, 107
RFP selection committee, 85
RGI units, 103, 104
Rivertowne, 28
Rogers Communications, 40, 41
Rose, Albert, 23

Rowe, Daniel J., 48
Royal Bank of Canada, 26, 40, 41

Saberi, Parastou, 75
safety, 59–62, 112, 125n31; of children, 68, 73; class privilege and, 73; conceptions of, 71; design and, 70–71; lighting and, 72–73; material design of spaces and, 125n28; as tool of neoliberal multiculturalism, 63; understandings of, 64. See also security
Sampson, Robert, 60
"Save Our Streets" campaign, 92–93
School Community Action Alliance Regent Park (SCAARP), 13
security, 125n31; design and, 70–71; revitalization and, 57–58; understandings of, 64
security state, 14–15
segregation, 3, 10, 17, 21, 24–27, 31, 35, 41, 43, 47, 49, 109; housing projects and, 37–38; Indigenous peoples and, 17; public housing and, 1; of Regent Park, 51; residential, 4; segregationist reserve system, 1; structural causes of, 106–7
settler colonial capitalism, 4, 12–13, 16
settler colonialism, 17
Sewell, John, 18
Sharma, Nandita, 5, 17
Sheila, 67, 68, 71, 101, 103
Sistering, 112
"slum" areas, 20
slum clearance, 20
Smith, Neil, 11, 12
Sobeys Fresh Co., 40, 41
social cohesion, 64
social development, 84
social development plan, 83–84
Social Development Plan, 84, 102
Social Development Plan (SDP) Stakeholders Table, 13
social diversity, 10
social housing, 26, 119n44; changes in housing policy in1990s, 44; federal

funding for, 111; federal government and, 26–27; funded by property taxes, 27; provincial governments and, 27–28

Social Housing Reform Act (SHRA), 27–29

social inclusion, 10, 38, 84. *See also* inclusion

social inequality, reproduction of, 16

social justice, 25, 109

social media hashtags, 61

social networks, 43–44, 49, 52

social policy agendas, 25

social regulation, 1, 3, 55–56, 108–9

social (re)production, 3

social risk factors, 32

social supports, 112

socioeconomic vulnerability, (re)inscription of, 3

Somali, 32

South Asian communities, 25

South Asians, 30

space, 59–60

Spalding, Ashley, 48

Spanish, 32

spatial (re)organization, 2

spatial design, behavior and, 60–61

state intervention, rearticulation of, 28

stereotypes, 69–70, 71, 93

Sterling, Mark, 62

stigmatization, 3, 24, 33, 41, 53, 67–71, 74, 81, 107; alternatives to, 105–6; class disparity and, 93; crime and, 66; territorial, 4

St. Lawrence redevelopment, 44

structural inequality, 4, 8, 106–7, 109

structural racism, 17

subcommunities, exclusion of, 82–83

subjectivity, construction of, 108

surveillance, 2–5, 10, 59–60, 109; construction of, 107–8; constructions of, 112; cultural diversity and, 63; definitions of, 107; diversity and, 14–15, 63; of low-income residents, 63; mixed-income framework and, 64, 65–66; nation and, 56; negotiated, 55;

64–71, 74–75, 76; neoliberal, 55–75; normalized, 3, 15, 55, 59–64, 66, 68, 71–75; participation and, 76, 107; revitalization and, 57–58, 71, 73–74, 76; three aspects of, 76

surveillance ideologies, 56–57

surveillance technologies, diversity of income and, 63–64

Syrian refugees, 8

Tamia, 68–69, 71, 76, 87, 88, 90, 93–94, 98–99, 103

Taylor, Charles, 6

Taylor, Harry, 80

Teelucksingh, Cheryle, 51

Tenant Advisory Committee, 85

Tenants First Plan, 34

Tenants for Social Housing, 112

tenure, diversity of, 45–46

Tesfaye, 105–6

Thatcher, Margaret, 5

Theodore, Nik, 10

Thobani, Sunera, 6, 9

Tim Horton's, 40, 41

Toews, Owen, 12

Toronto, City of, 13, 15–16, 18, 28–29, 44, 50, 129n1; adoption of consultation model by, 83; brief geographical introduction, 19; bylaw no. 17080, 21; City of Toronto Affordable Housing Committee, 83–84; consultation process and, 83–84; housing stock and, 87–88; lack of resources from, 76; *Lawrence-Allen Revitalization Plan* and, 33–34; public housing and, 28; Staff Report, 33; Tenants First Plan, 34. *See also* Toronto, Ontario

Toronto, Ontario: coat of arms of, 37; east end, 28; housing projects in, 17; Lawrence Heights, 1; neoliberalism in, 10–11, 26–34; as pinnacle of Canadian multiculturalism, 37; Regent Park, 1, 37–53

Toronto City Council, 32

Toronto City Hall, 25

Toronto Community Housing Corporation (TCHC), 4, 15–16, 23, 28–30, 32–35, 41–42, 44, 62, 66, 72–73, 102–3, 125–26n40; 2004 Annual Review, 30–31; accused of intentionally letting buildings deteriorate, 73–74; adoption of consultation model by, 83; communications and, 90–91, 99; consultation process and, 90–91; engagement and, 81–85; financial framework of "leveraging social housing," 29–30; housing stock and, 87–88; lack of resources from, 76; scandals and, 119n56; staff relationship with residents, 82, 86–87; unresponsiveness of, 99. *See also specific publications*
Toronto Development Department, Research and Information Division, 22
Toronto District School Board, 33–34, 83
Toronto Foundation, *Vital Signs Report*, 34
Toronto Housing Authority (THA), 22
Toronto Housing Company, 28–29
Toronto Metropolitan Housing Corporation, 28–29
Toronto Public Health, 26
Toronto Star, 1, 21, 42
Township of North York, 23
trans Black people, hyperpersecution of, 58
"transfer of public assets," 34
trans folk, 58
transparency, 101
Trudeau, Justin, 8, 58
Trudeau, Pierre, 8, 25

undercommons, 111
Underground Railroad, 6
United States: vs. Canada, 7, 16, 19–20, 27; housing policy in, 19–20; melting pot concept and, 7, 16; models from, 44; racism in, 7; revitalization and, 26–27; urban renewal in, 12; "war on drugs" in, 56; "war on poverty" in, 56

University of Toronto, learning center, 42
urban communities, investment in, 9
urban design, policing and, 15
urban development, neoliberalism and, 10–11
urban planning, 9–10, 79–80, 110
urban policy, 10–11
urban possibilities, 106, 112–13
urban renewal, 12, 19–20, 26. *See also* revitalization
urban revitalization. *See also* revitalization
urban spaces: culture and, 9; ordering of, 24; racialization and, 24, 25–26; separation of, 24
urban studies, 9–10, 11
use, diversity of, 14, 37–38, 39–43, 52, 53

Vertovec, Steven, 122n7
veterans, 21, 25–26
violence, 33, 61–62; built environment and, 62–63; Indigenous peoples and, 17; isolation and, 65–66; revitalization and, 69–70. *See also* police brutality
"visible minorities," 119n40
voting, 79

Walks, Alan, 49
Webber, Henry S., 43
welfare state, 25, 26; rise of, 18; rollback of, 11
welfare state policies: vs. revitalization, 107; shift from, 107
Wendat people, 19
West Indian, 32
"What We Heard," 84
White, Sealand, 72
whiteness, positioned as invisible, normative, or nonracialized, 2
"white-painting," 117n59
women's groups, 25

Woods, Clyde, 12
Workers Action Centre, 112
World War II, 8
Wynne, Kathleen, 8, 110

youth, engagement and, 84
youth outreach, 84

Zimmerman, George, 56

Printed in the USA
CPSIA information can be obtained
at www.ICGtesting.com
LVHW041135041223
765471LV00002B/137